Reimagining Lyric Diction Courses

Drawing on 30 years of teaching experience, author Timothy Cheek demonstrates how a university lyric diction class—traditionally specialized and Eurocentric—can become transformative, through engaging students with other languages and cultures, and promoting diversity, equity, inclusivity, and antiracism.

Raising new possibilities for traditional lyric diction pedagogy, this book explores how to provide students with experiences that speed their growth, help them to see the big picture, spark their curiosity, clarify and expand their digital resources and skills, and set them on a path of international collaboration. Arguing against compartmentalization in voice curricula, and exploring opportunities for creativity, the author provides a guide to new approaches that will aid schools' decisions about diction curricula in the challenging but promising era of 21st-century pedagogy.

Voice faculty, diction instructors, curriculum committees, graduate students in related fields, and music school administrators should all find this book insightful and thought-provoking as it goes to the heart of issues critical to the long-term development of today's voice students.

Timothy Cheek is a Professor of Performing Arts/Vocal Arts at the University of Michigan, where he teaches diction, Czech vocal literature, and is a vocal coach. In addition to work as a collaborative pianist, he is the author of seven books on lyric diction and opera.

CMS Emerging Fields in Music
Series Editor: Mark Rabideau, *University of Colorado, Denver, USA*
Managing Editor: Zoua Sylvia Yang, *DePauw University, USA*

The *CMS Series in Emerging Fields in Music* consists of concise monographs that help the profession re-imagine how we must prepare 21st Century Musicians. Shifting cultural landscapes, emerging technologies, and a changing profession in-and-out of the academy demand that we re-examine our relationships with audiences, leverage our art to strengthen the communities in which we live and work, equip our students to think and act as artist-entrepreneurs, explore the limitless (and sometimes limiting) role technology plays in the life of a musician, revisit our very assumptions about what artistic excellence means and how personal creativity must be repositioned at the center of this definition, and share best practices and our own stories of successes and failures when leading institutional change.

These short-form books can be either single-authored works, or contributed volumes comprised of 3 or 4 essays on related topics. The books should prove useful for emerging musicians inventing the future they hope to inhabit, faculty rethinking the courses they teach and how they teach them, and administrators guiding curricular innovation and rebranding institutional identity.

A More Promising Musical Future
Leading Transformational Change in Music Higher Education
Edited by Michael Stepniak

Reimagining Lyric Diction Courses
Leading Change in the Classroom and Beyond
Timothy Cheek

For more information, please visit: https://www.routledge.com/CMS-Emerging-Fields-in-Music/book-series/CMSEMR

Reimagining Lyric Diction Courses
Leading Change in the Classroom and Beyond

Timothy Cheek

First published 2023
by Routledge
605 Third Avenue, New York, NY 10158

and by Routledge
4 Park Square, Milton Park, Abingdon, Oxon, OX14 4RN

*Routledge is an imprint of the Taylor & Francis Group,
an informa business*

© 2023 Taylor & Francis

The right of Timothy Cheek to be identified as author of this
work has been asserted in accordance with sections 77 and 78
of the Copyright, Designs and Patents Act 1988.

All rights reserved. No part of this book may be reprinted
or reproduced or utilised in any form or by any electronic,
mechanical, or other means, now known or hereafter invented,
including photocopying and recording, or in any information
storage or retrieval system, without permission in writing from
the publishers.

Trademark notice: Product or corporate names may be
trademarks or registered trademarks, and are used only for
identification and explanation without intent to infringe.

Library of Congress Cataloging-in-Publication Data
Names: Cheek, Timothy, 1957- author.
Title: Reimagining lyric diction courses : leading change in
the classroom and beyond / Timothy Cheek.
Description: New York : Routledge, 2022. | Series: CMS
emerging fields in music | Includes bibliographical references
and index. | Identifiers: LCCN 2022039864 (print) | LCCN
2022039865 (ebook) | ISBN 9781032127743 (hardback) | ISBN
9781032127750 (paperback) | ISBN 9781003226208 (ebook)
Subjects: LCSH: Singing--Diction--Instruction and study. |
Singing--Instruction and study. | Culturally relevant pedagogy.
Classification: LCC MT883. C436 2022 (print) | LCC MT883
(ebook) | DDC 783/.043--dc23
LC record available at https://lccn.loc.gov/2022039864
LC ebook record available at https://lccn.loc.gov/2022039865

ISBN: 978-1-032-12774-3 (hbk)
ISBN: 978-1-032-12775-0 (pbk)
ISBN: 978-1-003-22620-8 (ebk)

DOI: 10.4324/9781003226208

Typeset in Times New Roman
by KnowledgeWorks Global Ltd.

To my friend Larry Hensel,
with gratitude and admiration

Contents

Series Editor's Introduction	*viii*
Acknowledgments	*x*
Introduction	1
1 Lyric Diction Classes for the 21st Century	4
2 The Role of Lyric Diction Classes: Laying a Foundation of Best Practice	15
3 Collaboration, Curiosity, and Creativity: Through Diversity, Equity, and Inclusivity	26
4 From Imitation to Communication: Best (and Worst) Use of Digital and Other Tools	40
5 From Compartmentalization to Transformation: Meeting New Challenges for Today's Singers	58
6 Virtual Exchange: A Window to the 21st Century	80
Index	112

Series Editor's Introduction

Emerging Fields in Music Series

Music is embraced throughout every culture without boundaries. Today, an increasingly connected world offers influence and inspiration for opening our imaginations, as technology provides unprecedented access to global audiences. Communities gather around music to mourn collective hardships and celebrate shared moments, and every parent understands that music enhances their child's chances to succeed in life. Yet it has never been more of a struggle for musicians to make a living at their art—at least when following traditional paths.

The College Music Society's *Emerging Fields in Music Series* champions the search for solutions to the most pressing challenges and most influential opportunities presented to the music profession during this time of uncertainty and promise. This series reexamines how we as music professionals can build relationships with audiences, leverage our art to strengthen the communities in which we live and work, equip our students to think and act as artist-entrepreneurs, explore the limitless (and sometimes limiting) role technology plays in the creation and dissemination of music, revisit our very assumptions about what artistic excellence means, and share best practices and our own stories of successes and failures when leading institutional change.

The world and the profession are changing. And so must we, if we are to carry forward our most beloved traditions of the past and create an audience for our best future.

Leading Change in a time of uncertainty and promise (a collection within the series) offers a comprehensive scaffolding of *why, what, how*, and *for whom* meaningful change is necessary if music schools are to equip students to invent the future they will soon inherit, offer faculty insights for rethinking the courses they teach and how they teach them, and recalibrate administrators' priorities, policies, and

Series Editor's Introduction   ix

procedures as they paint the new landscape of the 21st-century music school. The editor's premise for the collection is that institutions of higher learning in music must see their principal role as one that prepares musicians as one-of-a-kind artists-to-the-world, equipped with the requisite knowledge, skills, and understandings to create a lifetime of artistic moments, one after the next.

The collection begins by making the argument for music's "essential" place within the human experience as the foundation of professional and career development. It then offers and examines pillars for change by addressing three fundamental questions facing the profession:

Pillar 1: Whose music matters?
Pillar 2: What might be possible if we were to reposition creativity at the center of all that we do?
Pillar 3: How might individuals and communities, through the work of career musicians and the experience of music, become more joyful, hopeful, connected, and healthy through musical experience?

Each pillar opens with an anchor manuscript that provides a comprehensive approach for imagining change. Subsequent books within each pillar offer specific ways forward.

Finally, these books examine *how* the systems and eco-systems that drive our music schools maintain inequities and obstruct innovation. Examining the academic journeys of students, faculty, and administrators, the authors decode often invisible systems that limit our growth and offer opportunities to realign our words and actions with the goals of fighting for equity, fostering inclusivity, celebrating creativity, and embracing community and the joy inherent within music-making.

This manuscript, though situated within Pillar 1: *Whose music matters?*, simultaneously argues for repositioning creativity within lyric diction curricula. Cheek, over the course of this short form book, unpacks the history of lyric diction pedagogy and offers a new vision for the 21st century, one built upon diversity's ability to serve as our students' most influential teacher, technology's limitless (and sometimes problematic) usefulness within the life and work of emerging vocalists, and the phenomenon of virtual exchange as a means "*to spark students' curiosity, and help them develop a life-long fascination and love for other languages and cultures.*"

Acknowledgments

I owe thanks to many people who helped make this book happen. First and foremost, to all the students over the years from whom I have learned so much! Many thanks to my supportive and helpful colleagues across the University of Michigan, especially to the voice faculty, and especially to my chair, Scott Piper, who continues to challenge me to make a difference. Also especially to Louise Toppin and George Shirley, whose giving nature inspires us all. Thanks to Philomena Meechan and Todd L. Austin, expert leaders at the University of Michigan Virtual Exchange Initiative who go above and beyond in their inspiring work. Thanks to the financial support of the University of Michigan Office of the Vice Provost for Global and Engaged Education. Others at Michigan include Carlos Rodriguez, Whitney Peoples, Martin Katz, and Gillian Eaton. Thanks, too, to Mark S. Doss, Laurie Lashbrook, Sarah Meredith Livingston, and Angela Theis. *Grazie tante* to my Italian friends and colleagues, Anna Toccafondi, and Leonardo De Lisi and his amazing students who continue to embrace virtual exchange and African American repertoire. *Vielen Dank* to Susanne Kelling and her wonderful students from Germany, who embraced our exchange with enthusiasm and insights. *Děkujeme* to Ivana Mikesková and her wonderful students in Brno, Czech Republic. Special thanks to my wife Bohuslava and our son Tim, for their patience and understanding! Finally, many thanks to Mark Rabideau, all those at Routledge Books, and to my dear friend Larry Hensel, the prime mover!

Introduction

Reimagining Lyric Diction Courses demonstrates how a university lyric diction class, inherently specialized, skill-oriented, and Eurocentric, can become transformative—providing students with engaging experiences that speed their growth; help them to see the big picture; spark their curiosity; help to instill a lifelong interest in languages and other cultures; promote diversity, equity, inclusivity, and antiracism; clarify and expand their digital resources and skills; and set them on a path of international collaboration. The clear questions that are raised—questions for the 21st century—and the possibilities that are put forward, will hopefully aid various schools' decisions about diction curricula in our challenging, but promising new era.

The diction course that is described in Chapter 1 is one model, one possibility, for the 21st century. It is a class that, filled with optimal diversity and collaboration, blossomed to a whole new level when a virtual exchange component and a strong DEI element were added to the course. While advocating for international virtual exchange—one-on-one work with European voice student peers, with the study and performance of songs by African American composers as a major part of the exchange (Chapters 1 and 6)—this book also gets to the heart of issues critical to the long-term development of today's students:

- assuring best practice of diction pedagogy, as defined by a recent landmark study (Chapter 2)[1]
- freeing a diction class from siloing and compartmentalization by making it as diverse, equitable, and inclusive as possible (Chapter 3)
- guiding students in the use of excellent supplemental resources, mostly digital (Chapter 4)
- confronting incoming voice students' dearth of language study and lack of English grammar head-on, and finding a solution to avoiding deficit teaching (Chapter 5)

DOI: 10.4324/9781003226208-1

2 *Introduction*

This book illuminates pitfalls that have gradually been limiting and impeding the long-term development of native English-speaking singers in this century. When these trends are brought to light, and the right questions are asked—questions of antiracism, global collaboration, best practice in diction pedagogy, best use of digital resources, and equity, diversity, and inclusivity—it will be seen that we not only can meet the challenges of providing hard diction skills in a lyric diction course, but we can go much further. Transforming such a class also leads to an enhancement of digital skills, and to a profound development of the soft skills students need in today's world. These three skills all work together in a practical, experiential learning environment that is much more than the sum of its parts.[2]

We are almost a quarter of the way through our new century, and we are still finding our way, albeit with more and more hope, dialogue, and purpose. Why are our academic institutions taking so long to create truly relevant and significant changes that reflect the sweeping technological, social, and cultural transformations of this century? In *Beyond the Conservatory Model*, Dean Michael Stepniak and Peter Sirotin explain well that the incredibly complex and entrenched structure of academic institutions is made up of a large number of stakeholders who often have conflicting agenda. They also cite competing power and authority structures, a lengthy and complicated curriculum approval process, competition between academic institutions, which stifles communication and cooperation,[3] a tendency to support normative arguments over data-driven analysis, and budgets that reward the status quo over innovation.[4] One could also add limitations imposed by state legislatures, budgets that don't allow for sufficient diction instruction, or administrators who are not aware of current needs and challenges. None of this makes for easy change.

Yes, many institutions now have courses that fulfill a race and ethnicity, or a diversity requirement, absolutely fundamental for our society. Otherwise, many schools are tackling curriculum challenges from *without*, by adding outside workshops and outside guest lecturers. These are certainly extremely valuable and laudable. It is, however, time to address racism, DEI elements, global cooperation, and digital competence from *within* classes. The process doesn't have to be particularly radical, either—the transformation of the diction class described in Chapter 1 came about organically, naturally, as it answered one question after another.[5]

Introduction 3

Notes

1. Penelope Cashman, "International Best Practice in the Teaching of Lyric Diction to Conservatorium-Level Singers" (PhD diss., Elder Conservatorium of Music, University of Adelaide, 2019) Available at https://digital.library.adelaide.edu.au/dspace/handle/2440/120990.
2. Corey Seemiller and Meghan Grace make clear with extensive data that, although Generation Z is adept with digital technology, they need guidance in order to attain literacy. This is certainly true in lyric diction, where outside resources can seemingly serve as quick answers to short-term solutions. The best use of supplemental resources is explored in Chapter 4. Seemiller and Grace also point out that applied learning is preferred by many of these students. In a virtual exchange, diction concepts are quickly put into action with native speakers/voice students. Corey Seemiller and Meghan Grace, *Generation Z: A Century in the Making* (New York: Routledge, 2019), 203 and 204.
3. For better or worse, higher education institutions have become more business-oriented. Perhaps we should heed the advice from one of many of Jeff Bezos's famous quotes: "If you're competitor-focused, you have to wait until there is a competitor doing something. Being customer-focused allows you to be more pioneering." Too many schools are waiting to see what their competitors will do.
4. Michael Stepniak, with Peter Sirotin, *Beyond the Conservatory Model: Reimagining Classical Music Performance Training in Higher Education. CMS Emerging Fields in Music* (New York: Routledge, 2020), 68. Strategies for taking up change are explored in: Michael Stepniak, Jasmine Parker, David Cutler, Brian Pertl, and Kendra Ingram, *A More Promising Musical Future: Leading Transformational Change in Music Higher Education* (New York: Routledge, 2022).
5. Stepniak, with Sirotin. *Beyond the Conservatory Model*, 14.

Bibliography

Cashman, Penelope. "International Best Practice in the Teaching of Lyric Diction to Conservatorium-Level Singers." PhD diss., Elder Conservatorium of Music, University of Adelaide, 2019. Available at https://digital.library.adelaide.edu.au/dspace/handle/2440/120990.

Seemiller, Corey, and Meghan Grace. *Generation Z: A Century in the Making.* New York: Routledge, 2019.

Stepniak, Michael, and Peter Sirotin. *Beyond the Conservatory Model: Reimagining Classical Music Performance Training in Higher Education. CMS Emerging Fields in Music.* New York: Routledge, 2020.

Stepniak, Michael, Jasmine Parker, David Cutler, Brian Pertl, and Kendra Ingram. *A More Promising Musical Future: Leading Transformational Change in Music Higher Education.* New York: Routledge, 2022.

1 Lyric Diction Classes for the 21st Century

> Musical training is a more potent instrument than any other, because rhythm and harmony find their way into the inmost soul and take strongest hold upon it.
>
> (Plato)[1]

Advantaged by 30 years of teaching lyric diction, front line opera and opera workshop coaching (often with the same students), professional experience on the international stage as a vocal coach, collaborative pianist, lecturer, and author on lyric diction, and my own experiences as a student (a BM at a major conservatory, through MM and DMA degrees at major universities, all in performance), I have gained a perspective into the amazing strengths and inherent weaknesses of curricula and academia, with special attention on the unique nature of vocal studies.

Recently, I had the incredibly good fortune to experience firsthand a transformational lyric diction class that shows great promise for our era. I wish to share the outcomes of this class because I believe an examination of not only its content, but also of the organic way that it came to be, can be beneficial for schools in the midst of reexamining their long-established curricula. I hope, too, that this monograph will be useful for teachers of diction courses.

Since required lyric diction classes are very specialized, skill-oriented, and completely Eurocentric, they are usually made to fit neatly into a compartmentalized academic structure. For many schools, this structure has been in place for 40, 50, 60, or more years. The specialized study of lyric diction in a music classroom was, in the beginning, a radical innovation that needed to win over naysayers from within even the ranks of the National Association of Teachers of Singing.[2]

DOI: 10.4324/9781003226208-2

So, the very implementation of these classes was a great pedagogical leap forward for the instruction of singers and coaches.

But what about the needs of current and future decades of students? The students who entered into curricula 30, 40, or 50 years ago are not the same as today's students. Our current students enter college with very different skill sets, different strengths, different challenges, different needs, and a huge technological advantage that enables them to connect and collaborate on a global level. It is time to examine and question what is needed for today's students and what is possible in our hybrid era. The possibilities for growth are enormous. It is also necessary to illuminate and address pitfalls, since many are not even aware of them or their long-term effects on students' development. All assumptions, then, should be questioned. No longer can we say "Let's align our school's curriculum with peer institutions" in an era when many institutions are in the middle of reevaluating their programs at a very fundamental level. It should also be stated that, at this point in our music schools' changes, we must find ways to institute meaningful change from *within* classes.[3]

First, drawing upon a concrete example from my personal experience, I will show how a lyric diction course, when embraced for what it can be, is ripe for transforming academic curricula by homing in on what is possible when providing students with engaging experiences that speed their growth, help them to see the big picture, spark their curiosity, instill a lifelong interest in languages and other cultures, promote diversity and equity, and set students on a path of international collaboration and creativity—and all this from *within* a single class. Even a specialized, Eurocentric one. After examining how such a course is possible, I will then lay out questions to be asked, and pitfalls to be avoided.

When considering the results, I am all the more amazed, as this particular class happens to be an Italian lyric diction class, broadly regarded by diction teachers to be the most difficult of the three main foreign singing languages to teach.[4] It is also deceptively difficult for English speakers to sing truly well, as such vocal coaches agree that Italian consistently requires the most coaching time.[5] Over the decades, when diction colleagues have contacted me about pedagogical issues, or schools have contacted me about challenges faced within diction curricula, it has usually been Italian diction that presented the problem. The transformation that happened in my Italian diction class, though, can happen with any diction class. The main approach consists of asking the right questions and letting that guide our curricula.

6 *Lyric Diction Classes for the 21st Century*

Prelude: Technological Groundwork

Just before the pandemic began in March 2020, I was in the process of planning some carefully scheduled asynchronous lectures for my diction classes as a way of freeing-up class time for group work that would reinforce the lectures. (There is never enough time in diction classes!) Inspired by a teaching assistant who had recorded his lectures when he had to be out of town, I queried his students and found that they preferred these recorded lectures, as they could watch the videos on their own time and review any parts they found confusing. At this point in my planning, no one was yet aware of the encroaching pandemic. Now, of course, as a result of the pandemic, we are all familiar with the advantages of judiciously incorporating asynchronous lectures into our classes.

Simultaneously, a long-time Italian colleague and friend, Professor Anna Toccafondi, of the Conservatorio Luigi Cherubini in Florence, Italy, excitedly asked me to Facetime with her from Tuscany. She had worked in a summer program in Italy with a group of Korean singers, and the Koreans had made enormous progress, finishing the program singing in beautiful, communicative, formal Italian. The problem, she said, was that after singers return to their homeland and are back in their former learning environment, they regress from what they had attained in Italy. She was so right—this is partly from being surrounded again by one's own language and culture, and partly from returning to the structure of academia. Working with my own students in international summer programs and witnessing life-changing progress, and then working with them again in the United States in their diction classes, opera workshop, and opera, I could see how, after only a few weeks, the ingrained, compartmentalized structure of their classes, along with a more limited perspective and the pervasiveness of English, was erasing some of the impact of their European experience. No, they do not forget everything they learned, but they do not continue to take up where they left off, and they do regress. I was fortunate to be back with them, where I could remind them of what they had learned and try to place it back in context.

What Professor Toccafondi was so excited to tell me was that she had found a way to reconnect with the Korean students periodically to keep them on track and continue to build. She did this through Zoom, she said, and found it to be a great tool. Again, at this point, we were still clueless about the approaching pandemic.

Only days after this—still before the pandemic—I received a general email from our school's Virtual Exchange Initiative, offering

Lyric Diction Classes for the 21st Century 7

support and instruction to faculty for accepted proposals.[6] This certainly seemed like it was meant to be! I immediately thought of setting up virtual masterclasses for my Italian diction class with Anna Toccafondi, who then referred me to our mutual colleague, Professor Leonardo De Lisi, tenor, and Vice Director of the Conservatorio Luigi Cherubini in Florence, Italy. The Initiative's stipulation, however, was that the exchange had to be between our students and the other country's students, in which they directly worked with one another, and it had to be an equal exchange. This was going beyond the masterclasses that I had envisioned. The limitless possibilities ignited my imagination. So, since my colleague taught a class similar to my own, we decided that the exchange would consist of De Lisi's students helping my students with Italian songs and arias, and my students helping his with American songs. In between, my students and his would team up for short Mozart Italian recitative excerpts. The exchanges would be set up independently by the students, one-on-one on their own time outside of class. After the students' independent work together, we would then meet as combined groups for feedback and masterclasses.

Pandemic: Focus

Professor De Lisi enthusiastically joined me, and our proposal was accepted. Then, immediately, the pandemic hit. The long summer of 2020 commenced. In lockdown, I now had plenty of time to learn how to create my asynchronous lectures, and my Italian colleague and I received excellent instruction from the Virtual Exchange Initiative via Zoom. The pandemic brought our project into focus because, like you, we were compelled to experiment with technology and find creative, effective ways to teach. For so many searching for connection, at a fundamental level, the pandemic also brought us together in our common humanity.

On May 25, the public execution of George Floyd was seen across the world. Few would not be affected by this horrendous event and the wide-spread, long-entrenched injustices that it brought to light. Protests and a heightened awareness of racial injustice arose in America, and across the globe. Anti-racism must permeate all we do. Black Lives Matter. I asked my Italian colleague if he would consider assigning art songs by African American composers as the sole component of his students' exchange experience. De Lisi embraced the idea. Although the repertoire was completely new to him, De Lisi found it rich with variety, beauty, and depth, and suitable for a wide range of technical levels. He was excited for his students to explore these songs. Of course, most of my own students would be exploring

8 *Lyric Diction Classes for the 21st Century*

these songs for the first time, as well. They and their Italian peers would be learning them together.

Nothing can replace the detailed, disciplined work of learning new sounds, the International Phonetic Alphabet (IPA) that symbolizes them, and then working to communicate clearly and expressively in another language. I taught this foundational work the first half of the semester, almost as usual (virtually), given the pandemic. Then the virtual exchange commenced.

Selected students from my class worked online one-on-one with their Italian peers, on their own time, on their Italian song or aria. This went beyond a virtual masterclass (as wonderful as that can be), and even beyond what students experience in European summer programs. In many ways, it functioned as on-site experiential learning with peers. The students worked together on Italian diction, the meaning of the Italian text, style, and cultural and historical context. They took what they had learned, recorded their songs, and then presented them to our combined classes. We discussed what they had learned from the Italian voice students, much of which reinforced what we had been working on—"use phrasal doublings," "sing legato and drop in the double consonants," "don't forget long vowels," "this text is right out of Tuscany," "you need to distinguish between open and closed vowels," "this is a very special word," etc.—and then Professor De Lisi took over and delved deeper, masterclass-style. With the exchange, all my students' work was placed in context, they gained perspective, collaborated internationally, gained independence, forged new relationships, and crossed cultural boundaries. They grew exponentially because they were curious and engaged. And because they were so engaged, their retention was much greater. Not every student in my class was able to directly participate, but they, too, grew immensely and were inspired and motivated to work with their own partners on their recitatives, and to plunge deeper into text. All my students, too, observed Italian students' performances, witnessing another culture embrace our legacy of African American art song as part of an equal cultural exchange. Everyone was taken outside of their compartmentalized environment, their work seen in context, with a widened perspective.

I queried the students, asking especially if the experience was worthwhile for those who had not had the opportunity to collaborate with the Italians. Every single email response was affirmative, and here is a sampling:[7]

It was 100% worthwhile, there were so many things that I learned!

I think it is a great opportunity and such a creative way to take advantage of this unique period of isolation and online learning, and when the pandemic is over, this virtual exchange should most definitely continue to be offered.

I think this exchange is an extremely valuable endeavor. It was wonderful to synthesize the concepts we've been talking about throughout the term.

[The] class provided unexpected insight when listening to... how much further one can go textually.

I thought it was awesome!... When we revert back to in-person instruction, I think this is a collaboration that should definitely be kept.

From participants:[8]

Thank you for an awesome semester. Best diction class ever!

I felt this was my only course that took advantage of the online learning environment. Collaborating with the conservatory in Italy was genius...

...working with our Italian friends has been an amazing experience, and I have learned so much... I would love to do it again, or even work with singers from different countries in our other diction courses!

At our final joint Zoom class, Professor De Lisi spoke of how beautiful and substantial the African American songs were, and that it was a pity more people did not know about them. Then he announced that he had decided to program a special concert of American songs in Florence, with his students singing their songs by African American composers along with songs by Copland, Bernstein, and Ives. You can imagine the effect on my students. The unjustly neglected repertoire of African American art song had been placed on equal footing with songs by well-known American composers *and* with the Italian repertoire they had just studied.

A follow-up meeting with the Virtual Exchange Initiative revealed that Professor De Lisi's students, too, were just as enthusiastic. De Lisi spoke not only of the great cultural value and social skills that the exchange had brought about, but also the practical pedagogical value it had for his students—they had learned wonderful new repertoire with the direct collaboration of American singers, and they had advanced their skills singing in English, which would open up more job opportunities for them.

10 *Lyric Diction Classes for the 21st Century*

There was more great news, illuminating the rippling effects that had taken place on both sides of the ocean. And together we will explore the many-layered benefits of this exchange in the last chapter, along with details and updates about further collaborations. Of course, there had been misgivings going into the project, and these will be addressed, as well. For now, I need only state that my misgivings were all unfounded.

Diversity: The Key to Success

All evidence suggests that the optimal elements all came together to reveal that diction classes are ripe for this kind of transformation. One of those elements is *diversity*. My class consisted of a strong cohort of sophomores, some juniors, two senior music education majors, five masters voice students who had tested as needing the class, and three doctoral conducting majors. I usually have one to three first-year students and one to three collaborative piano majors, as well. I have found, without question, that this kind of diversity in itself enables so many different perspectives and so many opportunities for mutually beneficial collaboration and that a course of a single class level cannot come close to matching the pedagogical outcomes. This is all borne out in solid, plentiful research from the last 30 years (research that came *after* the establishment of many institutions' diction curricula, still in place!), along with recent research on diction pedagogy best practice, which will be explored in Chapters 2 and 3.

The benefits are enormous partly because the make-up of the class represents a microcosm of the professional world that the students will come to inhabit and prepares them for it. Professor De Lisi's class was even more diverse, with bachelor's and master's students combined, ages 19–40, and with students from eight countries, besides the Italians.[9] Put the two together, and we truly had a global representation of students interacting with their future colleagues. There was no compartmentalization in this combined class, no siloing, but rather a truly global community.

Over the years, I have asked myself questions about diction pedagogy, and all of them were answered in this exchange:

How to spark students' curiosity, and help them develop a life-long fascination and love for other languages and cultures?

These are the most successful singers, the most successful and fulfilled artists! This has always been a goal in my classes, and it will be seen from a recent study that this pedagogical goal is one of best practice by diction teachers worldwide.[10] As we will see in Chapter 4, if that fire is not lit, students usually develop a habit of simply relying on outside resources that provide IPA and translations, instead of attempting any of the work themselves *before* utilizing these great tools. As a result, they rise to a certain level but never progress further in the professional world. This will be explored later, as outside resources, most of them online, have an important role for this century when used to best advantage.

How can students better bridge the gap among learning Italian, German, and French pronunciation while isolated in an American classroom and direct communication in these languages in front of an audience?

A student, when singing in their native language, is almost always more direct than when they are singing in another language (unless they are bilingual). When I listen to students sing in a foreign language, I always try to imagine them within the context of singing for an audience of native speakers. No matter how connected they are, there is often a veil, sometimes thick, sometimes thin, between them and the audience. I found the real "ah-ha!" moments come when a singer is in Europe actually singing in the foreign language before an audience of native speakers for the first time. From then on, the veil is lifted, the singer is transformed. Singing in any language now becomes completely different. *Can that moment happen sooner, in the classroom?* I think we can now answer, Yes it can.

How to place a specialized, Eurocentric university course in context for the student, beyond the school's walls? And, can we shift the centrism to allow for even more layers of growth?

Through technology, this can be done. Sounds and translations can be brought almost immediately into context by connecting with foreign peers and communicating texts to them directly. Centrism can be shifted through an equal exchange, in this case through an exchange with songs by African American composers, further bringing students' work into perspective.

How to better engage students, further develop skills, and more confidently assure student retention of knowledge?

Students tend to enter college into compartmentalized environments, no matter how integrated our courses look on paper. They enter college ready to check off boxes and be finished with classes. They also tend to use their digital skills accordingly. A wider perspective and real integration are crucial.

How to widen perspectives, develop initiative, independence, and social and intercultural skills?

None of these goals needs to be shifted to outside workshops, as valuable as they are, or other classes. They can happen *within* a diction class. If they can happen within a class, why compartmentalize and

12 *Lyric Diction Classes for the 21st Century*

silo the class, when both the hard skills of diction and the soft skills of social interaction can complement and advance one another?

How to help lay a groundwork for a student's international collaboration?

This no longer has to wait for participation in European summer programs: Opportunities we know are not equitably afforded to all students. Collaboration through a virtual exchange happens with European peers who speak the language, instead of with a group of peers in a summer program who do not. For those fortunate enough to study abroad, the groundwork can now be laid beforehand, within their home institution.

Now, having experienced a transformational diction class in action, I am convinced that if we ask even more basic questions about diversity, equity, and inclusion, along with questions about students' needs in our new century, we can produce amazing results. Administrative considerations (the *when*, the *how*, along with *why*) can then be approached, instead of vice versa. There are also pitfalls to be aware of, and assumptions that must be examined. Here are the questions for diction classes that will be put forward and examined.

How can we be as diverse, equitable, and inclusive as possible?

How can we best make use of technology?

Whose music matters?

How can we best nurture curiosity and collaboration, preferably on a global scale?

How can we best foster independence?

How can we avoid compartmentalization and siloing?

For any choices made along the way, also ask:

At what cost? At what benefit?

What is the short-term vs. long-term growth? Are any long-term goals sacrificed for short-term goals?

Many schools are tackling curricular challenges from *without*, by adding *outside* workshops and *outside* guest lecturers. These have great value, but more crucial at this point in time is the question:

How can DEI and 21st-century elements be infused within a class?

Some of these questions at first glance may not seem to apply to such skill-oriented courses that focus on European languages. So, this rule should be applied:

Question any assumptions you make.

Notes

1. Plato, c. 375 BC, *The Republic*, Book III, Line 401d. Translated from the original Greek by Lydía Zervanos and used with permission, from: Plato, *The Republic*, includes both original Greek and modern Greek

trans. by I. Gryparis (Thessaloniki: Centre for the Greek Language, c. 375 BC/2015), at: https://www.greek-language.gr/digitalResources/ancient_greek/ library/ browse.html?text_id=111&page=39.

2. Cheri Montgomery, "Diction (Still) Belongs in the Music Department," *Journal of Singing: The Official Journal of the National Association of Teachers of Singing* 76, no. 3 (January/February 2020): 301.

3. Michael Stepniak and Peter Sirotin argue persuasively that the initiatives being publicly heralded at many institutions, though helpful, are "largely limited to the edges of curriculum," and "don't go anywhere far enough." Michael Stepniak, with Peter Sirotin, *Beyond the Conservatory Model: Reimagining Classical Music Performance Training in Higher Education. CMS Emerging Fields in Music.* (New York: Routledge, 2020), 14.

4. This is partly because IPA is so limited in capturing inflection, and vowel length is so crucial. The "Italian question" is explored in Chapter 5, and in Timothy Cheek and Anna Toccafondi, *Perfect Italian Diction for Singers: An Authoritative Guide.* (Rowman & Littlefield, 2022).

5. Vocal coach Marcie Stapp, of the San Francisco Conservatory, wrote: "[Italian diction] ... consistently requires the most coaching time ... Even the student who has spent considerable time researching and preparing the text may arrive with a barrage of questions stemming from disagreement among different sources." Marcie Stapp, *The Singer's Guide to Languages* (San Francisco: Teddy's Music Press, 1996), 87.

6. The University of Michigan's Virtual Exchange Initiative had been up and running since 2012, but I was barely familiar with it. See https://virtualexchange.umich.edu/about-us/

7. All quotes used by permission.

8. Quotes taken from completely anonymous student course evaluations.

9. Because of Europe's Erasmus+ program, European schools commonly have students from a variety of countries. This will be explored in Chapter 6.

10. Penelope Cashman, "International Best Practice in the Teaching of Lyric Diction to Conservatorium-Level Singers" (PhD diss., Elder Conservatorium of Music, University of Adelaide, 2019), available at https://digital.library.adelaide.edu.au/dspace/handle/2440/120990.

Bibliography

Cashman, Penelope. "International Best Practice in the Teaching of Lyric Diction to Conservatorium-Level Singers." PhD diss., Elder Conservatorium of Music, University of Adelaide, 2019. Available at https://digital.library.adelaide.edu.au/dspace/handle/2440/120990.

Cheek, Timothy, and Anna Toccafondi. *Perfect Italian Diction for Singers: An Authoritative Guide.* New York: Rowman & Littlefield, 2022.

Montgomery, Cheri. "Diction (Still) Belongs in the Music Department." *Journal of Singing: The Official Journal of the National Association of Teachers of Singing* 76, no. 3 (January/February 2020): 301–309.

14 Lyric Diction Classes for the 21st Century

Plato. *The Republic*. Includes both original Greek and modern Greek trans. by Ioannis Gryparis. Thessaloniki: Centre for the Greek Language, c. 375 BC/2015. Available at: https://www.greek-language.gr/digitalResources/ancient_greek/library/browse.html?text_id=111&page=39

Stapp, Marcie. *The Singer's Guide to Languages*. San Francisco: Teddy's Music Press, 1996.

Stepniak, Michael, with Peter Sirotin. *Beyond the Conservatory Model: Reimagining Classical Music Performance Training in Higher Education. CMS Emerging Fields in Music*. New York: Routledge, 2020.

2 The Role of Lyric Diction Classes
Laying a Foundation of Best Practice

> Do not confine your children to your own learning, for they were born in another time.
>
> (Talmud)[1]

Lyric diction classes for English-speaking singers in the American college music classroom began to appear in the mid-1960s, with a few appearing earlier. Some of the most renowned music schools, however, did not add lyric diction classes to their curricula until the mid-1980s. Before this period, foreign language lyric diction was studied through one's voice teacher, coaches, travel to Europe, books, or in language classes.

As stated in Chapter 1, at first, the very idea of a lyric diction class in a music classroom was considered unthinkable by many, even by some voice teachers functioning within the ranks of the National Association of Teachers of Singing (NATS). Many voice teachers at the time were not familiar with the International Phonetic Alphabet (IPA); and diction instruction for singers was mostly meant to take place in language classes, to be refined by the voice teachers. After all, this was the voice teachers' own experience, and it had worked well enough for them in their era.[2]

It was the implementation of IPA, in a somewhat simplified version pertinent for singing, that provided a foundation for a systematic way of teaching diction to singers, and it eventually caught on. The IPA and corresponding sounds were presented, described, and sometimes demonstrated with recordings in well-researched textbooks by experienced teachers: Madeleine Marshall, Berton Coffin, Ralph Errolle, Richard G. Cox, Evelina Colorni, Thomas Grubb, William Odom, and others. It was not enough, of course, to be armed with these resources, as the classroom diction teacher must find ways to guide

DOI: 10.4324/9781003226208-3

16 *The Role of Lyric Diction Classes*

students beyond the attainment of correct sounds, rule-learning, and phonetic renditions of songs to actual expressive communication. All of this involves finding tools that supplement IPA. A diction class requires a variety of pedagogical approaches, alternating between an instructor's presentations, the collaborative activities of students, the development of critical listening, and individual attention.[3] The usual format consists of studying rules, individual sounds and the IPA they represent, single words, and phrases in the first half of the course, and then a master class performance format in the second half, allowing for much practical, individual attention while benefiting the whole class and developing students' critical listening skills. There may or may not be one-on-one work privately with the diction teacher, as well.

Undergraduate Diction Curricula

The range of curricular layout for diction classes is very wide in English-speaking countries. For the four-year undergraduate curricula (three or five years in some countries), classes can consist of any of the following:

A   A one-semester introductory class that covers English, Italian, German, and French.

B   A four-semester format, one semester for each language.

C   A three-semester format, with one semester each for Italian, German, and French. German may possibly include English.

D   A two-semester format, with two languages covered in each semester. Sometimes English and Italian are first, using English as an introduction to IPA; then German and French together because of shared mixed vowels. Others use English as an introduction to IPA and combine this with German, because of the similarity of the languages;[4] and then Italian with French for the same reason. In either case, when this two-semester format is required during a student's first year, some schools correctly title the sequence as "introductory" classes. Very few of these schools, however, then follow up with more advanced diction classes.

E   A scaffolded approach to each language, so that, for example, there is an Italian diction 101, 201, and 301 (or 101, 102, 103).

F   Two semesters devoted to each language, with performances reserved for the second semesters.

G   Any of the above except A, with an added, usually shorter, introductory course for first-year students, that introduces singers to

The Role of Lyric Diction Classes 17

IPA—an "IPA class" (or "Phonics")—usually while comparing the sounds of the different languages.

H   A class combining language study and lyric diction, taught either by a language teacher or a diction teacher. This is now a rare combination, but some schools have either kept it in place after 50 or more years or have unfortunately been compelled to take this approach because of state-controlled credit restrictions or other factors.[5]

I   Schools in trimester systems adjust accordingly. For example, three languages in one year, three trimesters; or one language in one year, such as Italian diction 101, 102, and 103.

The number of hours per week varies considerably, and can be the subject of much contention and frustration, but is usually from one to three hours. If for one hour, the course is usually taken for one credit. If two to three hours/week, then for two credits. Larger schools of music need more time to be able to give enough individual attention to everyone. Common complaints, however, are that classes are too large, and there is never enough time! It will be argued that, because of current students' incoming needs, there is no justification for reducing the hours of diction classes—in today's climate (see Chapter 5), if anything, we should be adding hours—and certainly no justification for compartmentalizing the class and removing the ability to carry out best practices. (Imagine having to cut even 15 minutes from a weekly voice lesson!) Noted diction teacher, writer, singer, and voice teacher Cheri Montgomery represents many a music school with her plea:

> If the singer's art is to survive, then words, our most precious and intimately related topic, must be preserved. It is not acceptable nor is it responsible for panel members entrusted with the job of assigning accreditation to drop or limit diction from the singer's or vocal accompanist's curriculum. If too little time is devoted to the topic of diction, the hurried and labored attempts of the instructor become ineffectual. They have no recourse to give, as they feel responsible, adequate time to each language and are unable to reinforce the concepts introduced. Diction is not a lecture course; rather, it is similar to the lab setting of a piano class where students require one-on-one time with the professor in a group setting. Overloading sections is an exercise in futility inflicted upon the instructor by schools who wish to claim they have a diction program but are not willing to provide the necessary number of sections.[6]

18   *The Role of Lyric Diction Classes*

Nor does it make sense to limit the hours of diction classes with the justification that anything missed can be addressed in coachings or opera workshop classes, or that these can serve as the sole means of reinforcement. This is far from integration, but rather compartmentalization at its worst. The work in other courses should be reinforcing and overlapping with the work in diction classes, not attempting to supplant it. It may sometimes look good on paper and possibly satisfy a short-term goal, but the cost to students' long-term development is much too high. The curriculum, in this case, becomes more of "survival of the fittest." This will be explored in Chapter 5.

As for class size, I have found that large classes of around 20 students can thrive *if* the classes are as diverse as possible. Diversity will be discussed in the next chapter.

In her admirable study, *International Best Practice in the Teaching of Lyric Diction to Conservatorium-Level Singers*, Cashman concludes that the number of hours allocated to diction boils down to money on the one hand, and an institution's attitude of the importance of lyric diction on the other hand:

> The varying class hours allocated to lyric diction across the institutions at which the interviewees teach, or have taught, no doubt indicates varying degrees of budgetary capacity. However, it is also reasonable to conclude that such variation also indicates differing degrees of importance attributed by institutions to lyric diction tuition [instruction] within conservatorium-level singing studies. This is significant when considering the finding that conservatorium-level lyric diction tuition is essential to the development of the skills, habits, and attitudes that characterize professional singers who have excellent lyric diction, and that these skills, habits, and attitudes are of critical importance within the career-long continuum of lyric diction learning. Indeed, the continued development and refinement of lyric diction skills, and a singer's ability to implement refinements demanded of them in the professional context, may be career-enhancing where the singer possesses the other skills necessary for the profession.[7]

The above diction class formats may be part of the following curricula:

A   A **fixed** curriculum, in which students must take specific diction classes during specific semesters. In this case, English is usually first, or an introductory IPA class.

The Role of Lyric Diction Classes 19

B   A **free** curriculum, in which students are free to take any of the diction classes at any time during their four years.

C   A **flexible** curriculum in which students must take all the diction classes *by* a certain time but in any order that fits their schedules, interests, or strengths. The degree of flexibility varies:

1   By the end of the first semester of their junior year.
2   By the end of their junior year.
3   By the end of their sophomore year, the least flexible. If there are four diction classes, this is really A, a fixed curriculum.

D   A **mixture** of any of these, meaning that an introductory IPA class, or English diction, is required for incoming first-year students, and the remaining courses can fit into the structure of B or C.

How language study of Italian, German, and French fits into the various diction class formats also varies considerably.[8]

How diversity and compartmentalization play a role will be explored in subsequent chapters. For now, it suffices to point out the following.

The **fixed** curriculum is the least diverse and the most compartmentalized. It often occurs in music schools where students are less likely to pursue double majors. In effect, then, a fixed curriculum discourages double majors if that curriculum is too rigid. This inflexibility should be questioned in an era in which our schools are called upon to educate singers for professions that they themselves help shape. The importance of music institutions taking on this role was highlighted by leaders in arts organizations in a recent survey by Michael Stepniak, in which presenter Steve Wogamon stated: "With scores of less-satisfied musical graduates as negative examples, I have come to believe that the music curriculum needs a major overhaul, such that it becomes possible with the span of a reasonably-paced four-year bachelor's degree to complete two majors or degrees, of which only one is in music."[9]

The **free** curriculum has the potential to be the most diverse. It also more readily allows students to have double majors. Schools that promote double majors, then, often adopt a free diction curriculum.

The **flexible** curriculum also has the potential to be very diverse. Depending on the amount of flexibility, it allows students more to explore another major or minor, and so is a balance of sorts between free and fixed curricula.

The **mixed** curriculum has the advantage of joining incoming first-year students together for their required introductory IPA class (in this case, an advantageous use of siloing to help the incoming students'

20 *The Role of Lyric Diction Classes*

new college experience), and then moving them into more diverse classes in subsequent semesters. (This will be explored in Chapter 5.)

Master's (Postgraduate) Diction Curricula

Diction classes in a two-year master's degree program may consist of the following:

A Courses that explore the diction and vocal repertoire of other languages, such as Russian, Czech, or Spanish. These may be open to qualified undergraduates, as well.

B Advanced graduate classes in Italian, German, and French diction, with the possibility of English, as well. If these are offered, they are usually required for master's students.

C Review, or remedial classes in Italian, German, and French diction, specifically for master's students. Sometimes this is one class, sometimes three. Some schools require these courses no matter what the level of the entering master's student, in which case there is no B. Usually, a school will require them only if students test as being deficient through a proficiency/diagnostic exam. Some students must take both B and C, then.

D Some schools offer B (advanced Italian, French, and German), but not C (review classes). In this case, students who are not proficient in Italian, German, or French diction take the appropriate undergraduate class.[10] But then they must also take the classes in B if those are required—difficult to do in two years!

E Some schools prefer to combine the experiences of undergraduates and master's students if their diction levels are basically the same. In this case, if master's students are not proficient, they join the appropriate undergraduate class. If they *are* proficient, students are free to immediately explore A, and they further refine their skills in Italian, German, and French diction through coachings, voice lessons, opera roles, and further language study.

How master's students play a role in the development of 21st-century skills will be explored in the next chapter.

Best Practice

As of 2021, there is no kind of certification for teaching lyric diction classes.[11] Successful teachers come from various backgrounds, be they singers; vocal coaches; native speakers with a knowledge of

The Role of Lyric Diction Classes 21

formal, lyric diction, and how they produce the sounds they make; or a combination of these. None of these professions in themselves guarantee qualification or aptitude for teaching the classes. Besides knowledge, experience, and a gift for both classroom and individual teaching, the underlying prerequisite is a passion for languages, their sounds, their meanings, and the expressive communication of beautiful, emotion-packed words through singing.

The field of lyric diction pedagogy is so new that not only is there a lack of certification for teaching diction classes, but there is very little research literature on diction pedagogy itself. Excellent articles by Leslie De'Ath, Cheri Montgomery, David Adams, and others have appeared over the years in the NATS *Journal of Singing*. Recently, landmark research was carried out by Penelope Cashman, in her "International Best Practice in the Teaching of Lyric Diction to Conservatorium-Level Singers" (PhD diss., Elder Conservatorium of Music, University of Adelaide, 2019). Cashman defines "conservatorium-level" as university/college/conservatory level, and while her topic only slightly touches on curricula, she asks pertinent questions that are fundamental for establishing best practice in lyric diction pedagogy. In the 343-page document, Cashman also asks the most fundamental question of all, "What is the goal of a lyric diction class?" Once pedagogical goals and best practice are established through Cashman's findings, we can proceed toward how to support them through the structure of curriculum.

Cashman interviewed—almost entirely in person—noted diction instructors from esteemed schools of music across the globe. Because of time constraints, she centered on diction instructors teaching in the following schools: in North America: Juilliard, Manhattan School of Music, Mannes School of Music, Peabody Conservatory, Carnegie Mellon University, Temple University, and Cincinnati Conservatory of Music; in the United Kingdom: Royal College of Music, Royal Academy of Music, Guildhall School of Music & Drama, Cardiff/ Welsh International Academy of Voice, and Royal Scottish Academy of Music and Drama; and elsewhere in Europe: Vienna University of Music, and Amsterdam Conservatory. Freelance coaches in Germany and Australia were consulted, as well.

Based on the similar, candid responses of interviewees, Cashman identified five elements that can be seen to represent best practice in pedagogical style for university-level lyric diction teaching:[12]

Identifying and catering to each student's skill level
Diction skill levels usually vary widely within a class, even when all the students are at the same class level. In a mixed-age classroom,

22 *The Role of Lyric Diction Classes*

age is not an indicator of skill level, either, as a sophomore can easily have more advanced diction skills than a master's student![13]

Establishing trust-based relationships with each student and within each class

This goes hand-in-hand with the importance of diversity, equity, and inclusion and helps to build a team.

Providing well-timed and appropriate feedback to each student.

This comes with experience and aptitude.

Demanding a high standard.

Given the importance of communicating the text, this is self-evident! Professional standards for lyric diction, too, have never been higher.

Fostering in students a perspective of lyric diction development that extends beyond the period of their study, and providing the tools for that development.

This last element is extremely important. All pedagogues in Cashman's study iterated that the most successful singers are the ones who develop a lifelong passion for languages and expressive diction. Even singers with world-class instruments progress only so far if language is not a top-most priority for them, with very rare exceptions. It will be seen that, by centering curricular decisions on DEI and 21st-century pillars, this last crucial element can most effectively be carried out. Otherwise, the prevalent existing compartmentalized academic structure tends to work against a fostering of perspective and leads to a dependence on outside resources, especially in our era.

I would add two more elements for best practice to the above:

Laying a foundation of critical listening skills for diction.

This is one of the "tools" for lyric diction development mentioned above but warrants emphasis. Students need to be able to hear the difference between good and bad diction, and everything in between. They should also be encouraged to self-record and listen critically to their own diction before going to a coach for feedback. Besides the teacher's guidance, diversity of voice types and repertoire in a diction class helps to develop listening skills, along with the teacher's guidance.

Guiding students in the use of supplementary resources, especially digital ones.

Outside resources cannot become a substitute for diction knowledge and the attainment of communicative skills, with students

The Role of Lyric Diction Classes   23

becoming more and more dependent on them. They are great tools on the road to independence, and tools to help them refine their skills. Modern diction classes need to allow enough time for this guidance.

My own diction class syllabi have always stated the following as the goal of the classes:
"Clear, natural, and communicative expression." I agree wholeheartedly, then, with the consensus of all interviewees in Cashman's study when asked about the goal of diction classes. Specifically, they were asked how important, at the university level, was the teaching of expression and communication of meaning through lyric diction:

> They were unanimous in their conviction that communicating the meaning of a text while interpreting and expressing its emotional message is the goal of lyric diction and indeed of singing itself.[14]

Now that we have, at long last, an international consensus for the goal of lyric diction classes, and fundamental best practices for teaching it, we can ensure our curricula allow for pursuing this goal and best practice, and we can begin to ask more questions.

Notes

1. Madison Clinton Peters, *Wit and Wisdom of the Talmud* (New York: The Baker and Taylor Co., 1900), 64.
2. Cheri Montgomery, "Diction (Still) Belongs in the Music Department," *Journal of Singing: The Official Journal of the National Association of Teachers of Singing* 76, no. 3 (January/February 2020): 301.
3. This is a combination of lecturing, scaffolded teaching, and differentiated teaching, to be explored in Chapter 3. This type of class is ideal for promoting collaboration, creativity, and curiosity.
4. Amanda Johnston combines them in her excellent text *English and German Diction for Singers: A Comparative Approach*, 2nd ed. (Lanham, MD: Rowman & Littlefield, 2016).
5. Cheri Montgomery, "Diction (Still) Belongs in the Music Department," 308. See this article for why I write "unfortunately." Some teachers manage to do this well, but it is certainly not ideal. Best in this case is if the course is taught by a diction teacher who is qualified to teach the language, with plenty of time allotted!
6. Cheri Montgomery, "The Dynamic Diction Classroom," *Journal of Singing: The Official Journal of the National Association of Teachers of Singing* 68, no. 1 (September/October 2011): 59. Penelope Cashman discusses variants of class hours and respondents' satisfaction with the number of hours allotted in her landmark thesis "International Best

24 *The Role of Lyric Diction Classes*

Practice in the Teaching of Lyric Diction to Conservatorium-Level Singers" (PhD diss., Elder Conservatorium of Music, University of Adelaide, 2019), 198–200. Available at https://digital.library.adelaide. edu.au/dspace/handle/2440/120990.

7. Penelope Cashman, "International Best Practice in the Teaching of Lyric Diction to Conservatorium-Level Singers," 312–313.
8. How lack of pre-college foreign language study affects college diction curricula will be explored in Chapter 5.
9. Michael Stepniak, with Peter Sirotin, *Beyond the Conservatory Model: Reimagining Classical Music Performance Training in Higher Education. CMS Emerging Fields in Music* (New York: Routledge, 2020), 36.
10. The tremendous advantage of this approach is shown in the next chapter.
11. This does not mean that there never will be, however. Certification, as well as nationally standardized proficiency tests for incoming master's students, would help assure that schools establish curricula that meet standards for best practice. American teacher Cheri Montgomery gives her certification requirements in "The Dynamic Diction Classroom," 59. Canadian Steven Leigh, Ensemble Studio Lyric Diction Coach of the Canadian Opera Company, proposes his view of requirements in his "Testing an Approach to Teaching Italian Lyric Diction to Opera Singers: An Action Research Study" (MA thesis, University of Toronto, 2016), 9–13. Available at https://tspace.library.utoronto.ca/ bitstream/1807/72743/1/Leigh_Steven_A_201606_MA_thesis.pdf. Australian teacher, pianist, and vocal coach Penelope Cashman lists the necessary abilities of a diction teacher in "International Best Practice in the Teaching of Lyric Diction to Conservatorium-Level Singers," 149, 213–214. I myself would advocate for a requirement of some kind of fluency in at least one of the three languages.
12. Penelope Cashman, "International Best Practice in the Teaching of Lyric Diction to Conservatorium-Level Singers," 212.
13. This unique aspect of vocal development and training—that the level of one's vocal technique does not necessarily equate with the level of one's diction abilities and knowledge, even though technique and diction ultimately go hand-in-hand—is actually a great advantage for diction classes. This is explored in the next chapter.
14. Penelope Cashman, "International Best Practice in the Teaching of Lyric Diction to Conservatorium-Level Singers," 289.

Bibliography

Cashman, Penelope. "International Best Practice in the Teaching of Lyric Diction to Conservatorium-Level Singers." PhD diss., Elder Conservatorium of Music, University of Adelaide, 2019. Available at https://digital.library. adelaide.edu.au/dspace/handle/2440/120990.

Johnston, Amanda. *English and German Diction for Singers: A Comparative Approach.* 2nd ed. Lanham, MD: Rowman & Littlefield, 2016.

Leigh, Steven Alan. "Testing an Approach to Teaching Italian Lyric Diction to Opera Singers: An Action Research Study." MA thesis, University of Toronto, 2016. Available at https://tspace.library.utoronto.ca/bitstream/1807/72743/1/Leigh_Steven_A_201606_MA_thesis.pdf.

Montgomery, Cheri. "Diction (Still) Belongs in the Music Department." *Journal of Singing: The Official Journal of the National Association of Teachers of Singing* 76, no. 3 (January/February 2020): 301–309.

——————. "The Dynamic Diction Classroom." *Journal of Singing: The Official Journal of the National Association of Teachers of Singing* 68, no. 1 (September/October 2011): 53–60.

Peters, Madison Clinton. *Wit and Wisdom of the Talmud.* New York: The Baker and Taylor Co, 1900.

Stepniak, Michael, with Peter Sirotin. *Beyond the Conservatory Model: Reimagining Classical Music Performance Training in Higher Education. CMS Emerging Fields in Music.* New York: Routledge, 2020.

3 Collaboration, Curiosity, and Creativity
Through Diversity, Equity, and Inclusivity

> Creating an inclusive culture with a diverse mix of people rarely happens by chance.
>
> (Laura Hlavacek Rabideau)[1]

How can we best nurture curiosity and collaboration, preferably on a global scale?

Ten years ago, in 2011, diction instructor Cheri Montgomery wrote an article for the NATS *Journal*, "The Dynamic Diction Classroom."[2] She saw an alarming trend across the United States of schools eliminating or condensing diction classes, and Montgomery called for maintaining a full four semesters of individual English, Italian, French, and German diction classes. In many ways, she was a spokesperson for schools across the country, for only through a four-semester approach can best practice be carried out by the instructor, and only in this way can voice students receive the education they need. Since text is fundamental to a singer's art, inadequate diction instruction also affects the ability of voice teachers to utilize the limited amount of time they have in weekly voice lessons and affects the ability of stage directors to optimally carry out an opera workshop class. Vocal coaches are affected, too, as they try to fill in deficiencies instead of reinforcing diction and other work. This leads, basically, to survival of the fittest.

Most of Montgomery's (2011) article, however, is geared toward advocating for a diction class filled with collaboration and excited energy. For, when administrators are made aware of both the importance and potential of these classes, a compelling case is made:

> Have you ever walked into a classroom and immediately sensed that the learning environment was a place charged with interest and energy? Did you notice how students and instructor were

DOI: 10.4324/9781003226208-4

Collaboration, Curiosity, and Creativity 27

equally involved and enthusiastic about the topic?.... Our goal is to make the transition from teaching environment to learning environment through innovative classroom design, placing new emphasis on creative teamwork and collaboration.[3]

The emphasis on creative teamwork and collaboration is, in fact, ideally suited for a diction class. The very nature of learning sounds and communicating them means that every single class involves some kind of active participation from the students, whether as a collective, individually, or in small groups. A diction class requires a variety of pedagogical approaches, alternating among an instructor's presentations/lectures, the collaborative activities of students, the development of critical listening, and individual attention. Written work, spoken work, sung sounds and phrases, and performances are all important.

Diction classes involve both differentiated instruction and scaffolding. Both approaches involve teamwork. Differentiated teaching means that I tend to individual needs. Scaffolding means that we all take one step at a time, apply new skills in small groups, and keep building in this way until the students have the tools they need to progress on their own. A variety of teaching approaches are also necessary—visual, aural, tactile, physical, imaginative—because different people learn differently, and different people have different strengths.

Teamwork and camaraderie develop quickly, and they develop in an atmosphere of trust. This means that by the time students perform their repertoire in the class, they know they are performing in front of a supportive team who are listening attentively, curiously, and critically, in order to contribute helpful feedback, and in order to grow along with them. The supportive team and trust must be based on a diverse, equitable, and inclusive class.

Diversity, Equity, and Inclusivity

How can we make our diction classes as diverse, equitable, and inclusive as possible?

Laura Hlavacek Rabideau defines diversity and inclusion: "Diversity, in its simplest form, is all the ways that we differ from each other, including race, ethnicity, gender and gender identity, sexual orientation, age, religion, disability, socioeconomic status, education, and anything else that makes each of us unique. It also includes 'cognitive diversity' or different ways of thinking .... Inclusion puts diversity into action by fostering an environment of collaboration and understanding, where each individual feels respected and involved."[4]

28 *Collaboration, Curiosity, and Creativity*

DEI initiatives have been established at academic institutions internationally. We have a lot of work to do, but there is much hope in our ability to foster and cultivate a culture of respect, seeking equity for every individual person. Once our schools have done their best to recruit a diverse body of students, administrators, and educators, how can we further assure our diction classes are as diverse and inclusive as possible, and what does that do for students' education?

Inclusivity: Using Technology for Enhancement

Schools have support staff to help faculty provide equal instruction to students, including BIPOC and LGBTQ+ students, first-generation college students, and students with physical or mental health disabilities. For those teachers who wish to learn more about instruction for voice students on the autism spectrum, Dr. Rebecca Renfro is a frequent guest speaker on the subject, with her presentation "Singing on the Spectrum: Neurodiversity in the Vocal Music Classroom."[5] Given today's increased awareness, acceptance, and accommodations for the neurodiverse student population at the college level, there comes an increased responsibility for the classroom teacher to provide needed adaptations for voice students on the autism spectrum.

For students who are partially blind, large-print handouts are very helpful. For students who are completely blind, many diction instructors may not be aware of Cheri Montgomery's extremely valuable International Phonetic Alphabet (IPA) resources for readers of braille—online, digital resources. "Providing equal access to lyric diction resources and promoting inclusion in the classroom" were her reasons for creating a new phonetic system for readers of braille that enable them to write, send, and receive IPA texts via computer.[6] Through the use of a refreshable braille display (a device that allows braille readers to browse the internet, write and receive email, etc.), students who read braille can send and receive phonetic transcriptions of song texts by computer. Phonetic symbols sent from the student's device to the instructor, online, appear as standard letters of the alphabet that are very similar to IPA symbols. Instructors can send modified IPA texts to the student online, which are converted to braille on the student's device. Through digital technology and Montgomery's initiative and creativity, the great advantage of attaching a symbol with a sound is now accessible to singers who are blind, allowing them full participation in a diction class, with further avenues for exploring vocal production. A database of over 2,000 song texts in five languages

Collaboration, Curiosity, and Creativity 29

is available on Amazon, along with easy-to-read charts of the slightly modified IPA for the instructor, and other resources.[7]

For the singer with dyslexia, learning IPA can be especially challenging. I include here a description of the process from a singer with a Bachelor of Music in voice from a noted American conservatory. The audio she refers to has been available for decades; the video component is being used more and more in today's classes.[8]

> I found learning to read music and learning to use IPA equally challenging. The big support for me was the audio component. I needed to hear and see the symbol together a LOT before my brain could attach the symbol to the sound. It was the same for understanding the note placement on the staff, and learning to read words. I still find today that I cannot read a word I have not heard before. Ultimately, I have found that my success with IPA hinged on memorization. I needed to just know how to pronounce a word and then learn which symbol designated that sound. IPA was really just an additional step for my learning that I found to be (mostly) unnecessary. That is, until I was really proficient and needed it for studying Czech! Then I was very grateful I had mastered the symbols and sounds .... I think what could have helped me more would have been an audio track, or even video of someone making the shapes and sounds with their mouth.[9]

Equity: Whose Music Matters?

More and more of us are finding ways to incorporate great, unjustly neglected music into our classes, including music by women; as well as music by BIPOC composers, including African American composers. An English diction class is a great opportunity to advocate for the study and performance of art songs by African American composers (including great African American *women* composers!), as well as concert spirituals—to be studied and performed by *everyone*. In 2007, singers Caroline Helton and Emery Stephens published their thought-provoking article "Singing Down the Barriers: Encouraging Singers of All Backgrounds to Sing Art Songs by African American Composers."[10] At seven pages, it is easily assigned reading for an English diction class in preparation for what is always an important and needed discussion about race, America's history, style, dialect, ownership, and the role of the singer. Helton's and Stephens' article was expanded in 2019 for the important and timely book *So You Want to Sing Spirituals: A Guide for Performers*, by Randye Jones.[11]

30 *Collaboration, Curiosity, and Creativity*

While American singers spend years learning to sing convincingly and expressively in so many languages, even Moravian dialect, many shy away from the dialect in spirituals, or even spirituals that use standard English, even though spirituals are such an important part of America's heritage. A knowledgeable instructor can incorporate the diction of spirituals into an English diction class and encourage everyone to sing spirituals. It is also a good opportunity to introduce students to the biennial NATS Hall Johnson Spirituals Competition, as well as the George Shirley Vocal Competition, held annually since 2011 and devoted to the performance of African American vocal repertoire by everyone.[12] Students can also be directed to Louise Toppin's African Diaspora Music Project, which lists and describes thousands of songs and other works.[13] Great African American women composers should also be highlighted, such as Florence Price, Margaret Bonds, and Undine Moore.

Wonderful repertoire by African American composers can also be incorporated into a German diction class. Examples are the great songs by Robert Owens to texts by Hermann Hesse, Joseph von Eichendorff, and Hugo von Hofmannsthal. For a French diction class, there is the French song "Poème" by William Grant Still from his *Songs of Separation*, songs in French for countertenor by Robert Owens, and the wonderful Creole songs arranged by Camille Nickerson. Songs by women composers of *all* backgrounds abound in all languages.

Equity through Virtual Exchange

The renowned African American tenor George Shirley spoke about the University of Michigan's former spring term vocal program in Florence, Italy: "To have that experience, just for a month, alters the approach of these young people and raises their consciousness about Italian music and Italian culture in a way that four years of university study in the U.S. can't begin to approach."[14] This was spoken in 2007. Can we *now* begin to approach this within a university setting in North America and elsewhere, given the dynamic, innovative tool of virtual exchange? Virtual exchange evens the playing field, too, providing equity to all students in a diction class, not just those who have the opportunity to study abroad. This will be explored in Chapter 6.

Also presented in Chapter 6 is the possibility of having songs by African American composers be a vital component of the virtual exchange. This creates an engaging, multi-layered dialogue for everyone, further advancing equity in the equation.

Collaboration, Curiosity, and Creativity 31

Diversity: Ensuring the Key to Success

Let's go back to Laura Hlavacek Rabideau's definition of "diversity." There is one element that we should examine, and I will highlight it:

> Diversity, in its simplest form, is all the ways that we differ from each other, including race, ethnicity, gender and gender identity, sexual orientation, *age*, religion, disability, socioeconomic status, education, and anything else that makes each of us unique. It also includes 'cognitive diversity' or different ways of thinking.[15]

At some point in my teaching at the University of Michigan, I noticed the following phenomenon, and colleagues across the United States have shared similar positive experiences with me. Let's zoom in on an undergraduate diction class, which typically occurs during the sophomore year. Most schools plan the course to take place during this year, but even if a school has set up its curriculum on paper for the class to occur during students' first year, it rarely plays out that way, as first-year students have so many core courses to try and fit in during that time. So, typically, the class ends up consisting mostly of sophomores. Add to that one, two, or maybe three first-year students who entered college with exceptional piano and theory skills, along with, perhaps, advanced placement French, so their schedule allows them to take the course. The dynamics of the class already begin to change, as the perceptions and experiences of the two class levels and age groups are different. Add to that a junior or two, one possibly a transfer student, the other maybe a double major, or someone who for any number of reasons was just not able to take the class earlier. The diversity of the class has become even more enhanced, and it is almost guaranteed that the energy, engagement, attainment of skills—including critical listening skills—and the retention of skills will be exponentially enhanced for everyone in the class, as well. Those schools with free curricula (see Chapter 2) see this kind of diversity regularly; those with flexible curricula, a fair to frequent amount; and those with fixed curricula, rarely.

Now, if you have them, add to this class several master's voice students whose overall diction skills and knowledge are around, or even below, the level of the sophomores, and the dynamics propel to a new level, with all learning from one another and growing by leaps and bounds. This can happen because of the nature of vocal development, singers' backgrounds, and the different skills that singers must learn. The difference between a graduate

32 *Collaboration, Curiosity, and Creativity*

and an undergraduate instrumentalist is usually very clear. The difference between a graduate and an undergraduate singer is usually clear with regard to vocal technique and the maturity of their sound; but the difference is frequently blurred with regard to diction skills. In fact, a sophomore or even a first-year voice student may have more diction knowledge and skills than a master's voice student. This is a case where we need to make sure and take advantage of this circumstance, refrain from siloing the two groups, and add to the diversity of the classroom.

Finally, if we also add collaborative piano majors and graduate conducting majors to the class,[16] the increased diversity produces even greater results. Then, when we add an international virtual exchange element (and European classes are bound to be multi-age, as well—see Chapter 6), diversity and collaboration jump off the charts.

To further clarify this, let's turn to the landmark study by Penelope Cashman, *International Best Practice in the Teaching of Lyric Diction to Conservatorium-Level Singers* (see Chapter 2). Cashman writes:

> The interviewees' responses reveal a difficulty in distinguishing clearly between lyric diction tuition [instruction] for the undergraduate and postgraduate [master's] levels. In fact, this project was originally designed to explore only undergraduate level lyric diction tuition. However, it became obvious early on that fundamental lyric diction skills are often taught at both the undergraduate and postgraduate levels.[17]

In Cashman's study, teachers at top music schools internationally noted this range of abilities and knowledge, citing the nature of different singers' development and training and contrasting this with the training of instrumentalists. Interviewees noted how some master's students had problems singing single words correctly, while some undergraduates were able to quickly move to detailed inflection.[18] While some master's students' diction skills may be at the level of a sophomore, their vocal technique, however, is usually advanced, and *that* is the difference in skill levels. In Cashman's work, Kathryn LaBouff (Manhattan School of Music, Juilliard), Emanuele Moris (Guildhall, London; Royal Scottish Academy, Glasgow), and Valentina Di Taranto (Amsterdam Conservatory; Jette Parker Young Artists Programme, London) all state that the approach to the teaching of diction to master's- and undergraduate-level students *is the same*,[19] and this is my experience, as well, over the last 30 years. LaBouff and Moris summarized well that it is simply the repertoire of the students that provides the distinction,

Collaboration, Curiosity, and Creativity 33

with advanced singers singing more technically demanding repertoire. Speaking of her diction classes, LaBouff stated:

> I have the same [content] for undergrads as grads. The music gets more difficult and is more demanding technically, so I set the same groundwork for both and then how it's applied is based on the repertoire. It's more the requirements of the repertoire [that change] rather than giving [the students] different information.[20]

I have seen again and again firsthand how this element of technically advanced repertoire adds further to the pedagogical outcomes of a mixed-age diction class. Students are exposed to more repertoire, both undergrads and grads develop their critical listening skills, and everyone benefits from focusing on the unique diction challenges that can come with more vocally demanding pieces. Voice teachers recognize this value from a similar mixed-age learning experience that takes place during their studio classes. The difference from a voice studio class is that the focus is centered on diction. The development of critical listening skills—centering on diction—is a very important, best practice component of a diction class (see Chapter 2). This development goes far beyond the comparative listening of recordings, because the diction class work is immediate, live, and provides feedback and corrections made in the moment. Cashman concludes by summarizing "... there was universal acknowledgement of the range of lyric diction ability and experience evident amongst undergraduate and postgraduate [master's] students. This range contributes to a blurring of the two educational levels, making it very difficult to create a clear pedagogical distinction between undergraduate and postgraduate tuition [master's level instruction]."[21] Those master's students who are already proficient, of course, go on to explore other languages, and to refine their French, Italian, German, and English diction skills in their voice lessons, coachings, and opera.

Plentiful research on multi-age college classes affirms the great value of allowing and even planning for this kind of diversity to occur. It is telling that, although this research goes back decades, it was mostly carried out *after* many universities had set up their diction curricula.

A study from 2017 examines much of the literature and finds that *both* older (defined in this study as 25 years old and older) and younger students "consistently indicate that they value, prefer, and learn more in mixed-age classes than age-segregated classes and that mixed-age classes help them see different perspectives."[22] Looking toward the needs of the new century, Debra Fair in 2000 wrote that

34   Collaboration, Curiosity, and Creativity

"The studies reveal agreement among the faculty, older students, and younger students that older students contribute and enhance the educational experience .... Both groups learn some things that lie beyond course content."[23] What are some of those "things"? Fair mentions that older students help give younger ones a perspective, values, and goals, helping them to see that education is a lifelong endeavor.[24] I would say, as an example, that while some undergraduate students are ready to check off a box and be finished with a diction class, they learn from their older colleagues that the class is actually the beginning of a lifelong passion for diction and language study. I would also argue that the older students are learning from the younger ones, too, because of their different perspectives. Fair also reminds us that "... the multi-age classroom has become the norm in the college setting."[25] So, whether it is an English class or an Italian 101 language class, this is nothing new for students, and they consistently prefer it that way. Faculty do, too, because they see the huge difference in motivation, and in the acquisition and retention of skills. Colleagues, whose schools are limited to undergraduates in their diction classes, tell me that those schools that can add master's students to the mix are very lucky, because the students grow so much. I have one musical theater colleague who describes an all-sophomore class as "myopic." When I have taught such myopic diction classes, the energy and effectiveness of the class cannot compare with one that is as diverse as possible. To me, such a highly diverse class produces results ten-fold over a single-class level, no matter how small the latter class is.

While "ten-fold" is my personal impression, Laura Hlavacek Rabideau cites a more precise statistic from the business world: "Deloitte Australia research shows that inclusive teams outperform their peers by 80 percent in team-based assessments, clearly demonstrating the power of creating a culture where all voices are heard and valued."[26] "Inclusion puts diversity into action by fostering an environment of collaboration and understanding, where each individual feels respected and involved," notes Rabideau.[27] A diverse diction class quickly becomes a team of supportive students learning from one another, in an environment that develops the soft skills that will help them to thrive in the professional world.

"Creating an inclusive culture with a diverse mix of people rarely happens by chance."[28] If voice students with the same basic diction skill levels in such a diverse setting can outperform a myopic group by 80% (or even 50, 30, or 20%!), shouldn't we make it happen? It can happen by not siloing master's students who need the class, and not siloing undergraduates past their first or second semester.

Collaboration, Curiosity, and Creativity 35

Here are the advantages of a mixed-age diction class, a result of what Cashman called the "blurring of the two educational levels," master's and undergraduate, when their diction skills and knowledge levels are similar. When conducting majors and collaborative piano majors are added—some of whom are considerably older—diversity is further enhanced. Let's keep in mind that students in diction classes inherently benefit from the small-group collaboration that takes place, in addition to the masterclass performance setting, with feedback from all, so there really is a true interaction of mixed ages here:

1 Students' **critical listening skills** are much more acutely developed, which is a fundamental, best practice objective of a diction class. From learning to critically listen to basic diction concepts to more complex, detailed combinations of sounds to challenges that arise in more technically advanced repertoire, everyone benefits from hearing a **wide variety of repertoire** sung by classmates. While the comparative listening of recordings is important, this goes far beyond that, as the performances are live and immediate. Corrections and different approaches are made on the spot, with the immediate input and feedback of a team (the class). Plus, the established camaraderie and support of the class while students of different ages perform for one another further enhances the benefits of the class, as follows.

2 Students from different age groups have a much **greater perspective** and understanding of their colleagues. This contributes to **cooperation** and an atmosphere of **mutual respect**, very important for students' lives and their profession. Why wait for other classes for this to happen? Why separate and remove this crucial aspect from a class?

3 Students learn **communication skills** when paired with colleagues that encompass a wider age group. They gain important **social skills** for life **outside of the conservatory environment** as they will interact with people of all ages and backgrounds beyond their time within the academy.

4 They will all learn different perspectives, from the entire age spectrum, younger and older, that they WOULD NOT HAVE HAD in an ordinary curriculum. This also **fosters inclusivity** in a classical music arena.

5 Students are more engaged, **more curious**, in such a diverse class. Energy feeds on itself, so that students learn more, learn more quickly, and retain more.

6 A mixed-age college class is nothing new for most master's students, as it became **the norm** at the undergraduate level decades ago. They will have already experienced it in language classes,

36　*Collaboration, Curiosity, and Creativity*

writing classes, and elsewhere. Most will be comfortable with the setting from the beginning and eager to soak up every detail in order to be on top of their diction skills and knowledge.

7　A substantial number of master's voice students will teach private voice lessons as part of their freelance careers, or already do. They eagerly absorb **new insights** learned from the younger students and excitedly absorb **new teaching approaches** that they observe from the instructor. These are different approaches than they learn in a vocal pedagogy class. This aspect has been frequently conveyed to me by master's students in my classes.

8　Master's voice students can sometimes be called upon to explain and demonstrate to the rest of the class how they first learned to roll an *r*, to explain what is a glottal, etc. While **raising their confidence level** and their awareness of what is expected of them, it also makes them think and verbalize what they are actually doing to make certain sounds, **adding to their skill level and knowledge**.

9　A mixed-age class, especially if it also includes conductors and pianists, is **a microcosm, or mirror of the professional world** the students will be entering. The interaction of younger and older; of singers, conductors, and pianists; all sharing the same goals and interests, working together to learn and grow, is part of a formula for success—not only with diction skills, but also in life. Why remove this element when you can add it?

10　Diction instruction involves a sensitivity to both the needs of individuals and the group as a whole. A more diverse group means that there are **more ways for students to learn from one another**. With this kind of vibrant energy, a large class, 20–23, is manageable in this case! Otherwise, a "myopic" group of, say, only sophomores, all the same age, becomes challenging over 12 students or so, and even with a smaller size class, the results are not nearly as effective.

11　The older students **instill a sense of value** to the younger students, a realization that diction and language skills are part of a lifelong journey, not skills to be checked off along the road to a diploma. A siloed class of first-year or second-year students would not receive this super-important perspective.

12　Older students **gain clarity and insight** as they learn some basic skills for the first time, **refine** other skills, and **discover** new approaches and new perspectives. Along with younger students, they see and learn much more, at many levels, than if they had been isolated/siloed with their own age group. The master's students can leave the class with **confidence** knowing they have fully tackled a weakness and emerged with a **strength**.

Collaboration, Curiosity, and Creativity 37

I could go on, as greater diversity, like collaboration, produces ever-widening waves of positive outcomes. When we then move to an international virtual exchange (see Chapter 6), the outcomes seem limitless.

Notes

1. Quote used with permission. Mark Rabideau, *Creating the Revolutionary Artist: Entrepreneurship for the 21st-Century Musician* (Lanham, MD: Rowman & Littlefield, 2018), 75.
2. Cheri Montgomery, "The Dynamic Diction Classroom," *Journal of Singing: The Official Journal of the National Association of Teachers of Singing* 68, no. 1 (September/October 2011): 53–60.
3. Ibid., p. 53.
4. Rabideau, *Creating the Revolutionary Artist*, 74.
5. Dr. Renfro is a Professor of Voice and Director of Opera Workshop at Sam Houston State University and can be contacted at rlrenfro@shsu.edu.
6. Cheri Montgomery, "IPA Braille for Lyric Diction: A Mutually Accessible Phonetic System for Teachers and Students," *Journal of Singing: The Official Journal of the National Association of Teachers of Singing* 77, no. 2 (November/December 2020): 227.
7. For information, see Montgomery, "IPA Braille for Lyric Diction," 219–232.
8. The University of Iowa's "Sounds of Speech" website is useful for most everyone, not just those with dyslexia—their free webpages feature animations, videos, and audio, all while simultaneously seeing IPA, for all the sounds in German and Spanish. (A separate mobile app is available for American English.) See "Sounds of Speech," University of Iowa, accessed September 21, 2021, https://soundsofspeech.uiowa.edu/german. With their video tutorials, *The Diction Police* website also takes the lead in this regard, especially for French Diction: François Germain and Ellen Rissinger, *The Diction Police*, accessed on May 18, 2021, https://www.dictionpolice.com.
9. Email to the author, May 26, 2021. Used with permission.
10. Caroline Helton and Emery Stephens, "Singing Down the Barriers: Encouraging Singers of All Backgrounds to Sing Art Songs by African American Composers," *New Directions for Teaching and Learning* no. 111 (Fall 2007): 73–79. Available at https://deepblue.lib.umich.edu/bitstream/handle/2027.42/57353/288_ftp.pdf?sequence=1.
11. Randye Jones, *So You Want to Sing Spirituals: A Guide for Performers* (Lanham, MD: Rowman & Littlefield, 2019), 144–161.
12. The NATS competition is at https://www.nats.org/Hall_Johnson_Spirituals_Competition.html. The George Shirley competition is at https://georgeshirleycompetition.org.
13. At https://africandiasporamusicproject.org.
14. Marilou Carlin, "Retirements," *Michigan Muse* 40, no. 2 (Spring 2007): 37.
15. Rabideau, *Creating the Revolutionary Artist*, 74.
16. See Montgomery, "The Dynamic Diction Classroom," 58.

38　*Collaboration, Curiosity, and Creativity*

17. Penelope Cashman, "International Best Practice in the Teaching of Lyric Diction to Conservatorium-Level Singers" (PhD diss., Elder Conservatorium of Music, University of Adelaide, 2019), 207. Available at https://digital.library.adelaide.edu.au/dspace/handle/2440/120990.
18. Ibid., pp. 206–210. Also noted was that knowledge of IPA is no indicator of sung diction skills. Also, some master's students do not know IPA, especially international students, while undergraduates may very well know IPA from pre-college work, an introductory IPA class, or another diction class.
19. Ibid., p. 209.
20. Ibid., p. 210.
21. Ibid.
22. Adam G. Panucci, "Adult Students in Mixed-Age Postsecondary Classrooms: Implications for Instructional Approaches," *The College Quarterly* 20, no. 2 (2017): 1.
23. Debra Fair, "Factors Associated with Participation of Learners in College Freshman Multi-Age Classes," (PhD diss., University of Georgia, 2000), 44.
24. Ibid., p. 48.
25. Ibid., p. 139.
26. Rabideau, *Creating the Revolutionary Artist*, 75.
27. Ibid., p. 74.
28. Ibid., p. 75.

Bibliography

Carlin, Marilou. "Retirements." *Michigan Muse* 40, no. 2 (Spring 2007): 37.

Cashman, Penelope. "International Best Practice in the Teaching of Lyric Diction to Conservatorium-Level Singers." PhD diss., Elder Conservatorium of Music, University of Adelaide, 2019. Available at https://digital.library.adelaide.edu.au/dspace/handle/2440/120990.

Fair, Debra. "Factors Associated with Participation of Learners in College Freshman Multi-Age Classes." PhD diss., University of Georgia, 2000.

"George Shirley Vocal Competition. African American Vocal Repertoire." www.georgeshirleycompetition.com.

Germain, François, and Ellen Rissinger. "The Diction Police." Accessed May 18, 2021. https://www.dictionpolice.com.

Helton, Caroline, and Emery Stephens. "Singing Down the Barriers: Encouraging Singers of All Backgrounds to Sing Art Songs by African American Composers." *New Directions for Teaching and Learning* 2007, no. 111 (Fall 2007): 73–79. Available at https://deepblue.lib.umich.edu/bitstream/handle/2027.42/57353/288_ftp.pdf?sequence=1

Jones, Randye. *So You Want to Sing Spirituals: A Guide for Performers*. Lanham, MD: Rowman & Littlefield, 2019.

Montgomery, Cheri. "The Dynamic Diction Classroom." *Journal of Singing: The Official Journal of the National Association of Teachers of Singing* 68, no. 1 (September/October 2011): 53–60.

_____. "IPA Braille for Lyric Diction: A Mutually Accessible Phonetic System for Teachers and Students." *Journal of Singing: The Official Journal of the National Association of Teachers of Singing* 77, no. 2 (November/December 2020): 219–232.

"NATS Hall Johnson Spirituals Competition." https://www.nats.org/Hall_Johnson_Spirituals_Competition.html

Panucci, Adam G. "Adult Students in Mixed-Age Postsecondary Classrooms: Implications for Instructional Approaches." *The College Quarterly* 20, no. 2 (2017): 1.

Rabideau, Mark. *Creating the Revolutionary Artist: Entrepreneurship for the 21st-Century Musician.* Lanham, MD: Rowman & Littlefield, 2018.

Toppin, Louise. "African Diaspora Music Project." https://africandiasporamusicproject.org.

University of Iowa. "Sounds of Speech." Accessed September 21, 2021. https://soundsofspeech.uiowa.edu/german.

4 From Imitation to Communication

Best (and Worst) Use of Digital and Other Tools

From infancy, we learn by observing, imitating, and repeating. Some call this "rote" learning, using a word that has largely negative connotations because of its mechanical aspect. Obviously, though, rote learning has its place in our development and ability to advance. Shinichi Suzuki based his revolutionary system of violin teaching on our natural acquisition of language through hearing, imitating, and repeating. In the book *Outliers*, Malcolm Gladwell demonstrated the phenomenon of 10,000 hours of practice, training, and exploration as a condition for success for athletes, musicians, computer science pioneers, and others.[1]

For foreign lyric diction, correct sounds must first be heard. Moreover, their formation must also be clearly described, felt, and understood, because attempts at mere imitation will usually result in producing the nearest equivalent in one's own language. Symbols from the International Phonetic Alphabet (IPA) are assigned to each sound. With this knowledge, physical sensation, IPA symbol, and aural model, a student can then put in the hours (10,000?) of focused repetition to build a new area in the brain for the sounds, words, and inflection of each language.

The goal of imitation and repetition is comprehension, assimilation, and especially in the case of music-making, expressive communication. Suzuki's imitation was always purposeful, with musicality, beautiful tone, and expression taught from the beginning. Gladwell's examples of 10,000 hours are all also purposeful and largely experiential. We would all do well to keep in mind the philosophy of composer Leoš Janáček, as described by Czech writer Milan Kundera: "only the note that is expression, that is emotion, has the right to exist."[2] At what point in voice students' training can singers move from imitation to communication, and what is the best way to make use of modern tools to help in this goal?

DOI: 10.4324/9781003226208-5

From Imitation to Communication 41

There are different ways of working on the mechanical, physical production of making foreign sounds and stringing them together in phrases and sentences. I like to ask my students how soon in this process can they begin connecting with the emotional meaning behind these sounds and words, so that, for example, *orribile* cannot help but to always have an expressive rolled *r*; or *dolor* will always have closed [o]'s, a single [l], and a rolled [rr] (when the word is final) because that is how it feels when we express sorrow in Italian.

There are many ways of working on the expressive communication of text side-by-side with learning the production of mechanical sounds. These ways are explored by each individual singer throughout their career, and students can be introduced to some of them by their voice teachers, diction teachers, coaches, and stage directors. By adhering to best practice in the goals of a diction class, the class *must* include a process for learning the physical production of correct sounds, an understanding of when to make those sounds, *and* the active engagement of connecting with text, spoken and sung, to communicate expressively. The latter is the goal of singing, the common denominator among the voice department's team. Keeping the goal in mind, and reminding students of the goal, keeps us mindful of the essential importance of course integration. If a diction class stops with only correct, mindless, and heartless sounds, it becomes compartmentalized, students do not retain rules, and they rely on outside resources for IPA, pronunciation, and translations. Expecting mindless sounds to be brought into context completely through another class, a voice lesson, or a coaching tackles the problem from the wrong direction, eliminating any hopes of integrating student learning across courses.

What are some of the tools at a modern singer's disposal for connecting with text? They are a combination of traditional and ever-expanding digital tools, from a vocal coaching to IPA to self-recording to YouTube to DictionBuddy, to name just a few. New tools are sure to follow. The pitfall for their use is that they can become ends in themselves or attempts at shortcuts that replace and omit parts of the learning process. The compartmentalization of classes, and diction classes that do not or cannot carry out best practice, sets up the use of tools as replacements for students' work or knowledge, which can easily have ramifications years down the road. Here is one example.

An incoming *doctoral* voice student demonstrated outstanding proficiency in both his written proficiency ("diagnostic") diction tests and his singing. An intelligent and polished performer with a beautiful, expressive voice, and a recent graduate of a top-notch master's

42 *From Imitation to Communication*

program, he impressed me with his written diction knowledge and vocal abilities. When cast in an Italian opera later in the year, however, he confided in me that he had no idea how to look up the pronunciation of Italian stressed *e*'s and *o*'s. Nor was he able to provide a translation for verbs ending in *-ea*—his dictionary didn't help, and the online resources he used didn't recognize these archaic, poetic forms. There were other issues, as well, such as improper stresses and occasional troubles with lining up triphthongs and double diphthongs, and finding the long vowel in these clusters.

How could this be? His background included an undergraduate diction class (four languages in two semesters, taken during the sophomore year); an Italian language class; a required master's level Italian diction review class at an esteemed college of music at a renowned university; and two years of graduate work with outstanding coaches, whose work I know well and highly regard. *Plus*, he had passed my proficiency test with flying colors! How was this possible? His reply was that, although he learned the rules, he did not know how to apply them, and that in all his work singing in Italian up to this point he had used preexisting resources that provided IPA and translations. No resources, however, existed for his current role, and this was the first time this had occurred. In addition, he said, his required master's level review class did not go into enough basic, practical detail.

In actuality, it was beneficial that these issues came to light, otherwise he could have graduated with a doctorate before anyone actually knew he was incapable of doing the work himself.

There are several issues here: shortcomings in his siloed undergraduate course; limitations of a siloed master's level review class; the fact that Italian language classes don't cover common grammatical features of Italian libretti; the singer's seeming lack of initiative in seeking help from his voice teacher or coaches to clear up these gaps; and the fact that no one seemed to notice the student's deficiencies (including myself!). A fundamental problem, too, is America's lack of language instruction, and the elimination of most grammar instruction, setting singers off on the wrong foot from the start (see Chapter 5). All of these need to be addressed, but the obvious overreliance on outside resources and coachings for his Italian diction and translations is especially telling. This is definitely not an isolated case. In fact, a recently published diction book overtly tells the voice student to find one of many preexisting translations and IPA for their songs and to use these to learn their texts and pronunciation. So, while some students fall into the trap of becoming completely reliant on these resources, other students are taught to be reliant!

From Imitation to Communication   43

Of course, if our goal is to teach singers IPA so that they can simply read preexisting material, we can simplify our classes, even forget about diction rules, and let coaches supply inflection, expression, and—if there are none to be found—translations and IPA. But this is not an uncommon language. This is Italian, *the* language of singing! Is this the new 21st-century singer that you would want to be?

We have already established the crucial pedagogical element for best practice through Cashman's study (Chapter 2): *Fostering in students a perspective of lyric diction development that extends beyond the period of their study, and providing the tools for that development.*[3] In other words, helping to create a spark that ignites a lifelong study of text in various languages by tapping into students' innate curiosity and desire to excel.

Cashman further reports:

> Though all the interviewees acknowledged that the luxury of extended preparation time is not always possible in the singing profession, they noted the discipline of those singers who have excellent lyric diction, regardless of time constraints. Radcliffe spoke with some exasperation of those students and professionals who do not undertake the process of 'opening a score, going to the words [and] translating the words' before they begin singing. She noted that those who use language best in their singing, 'translate the whole bloody opera—they don't just translate their bit.' She described this as a discipline, and an act of prioritization, saying, 'They do it first, and they always do it, and they won't cheat, and they won't cut corners.' Radcliffe emphasized that this process is vital to achieving high quality lyric diction.[4]

Those professional singers who do not make this kind of work a priority—an act of tenacity—almost certainly fail to rise beyond a certain point.[5]

What would lead a singer to rely on other people's work? Certainly, the time pressure (as noted above), which is undeniable in their profession and studies. Outside resources save time and can save money, too. But if there is enough time to delve into a text and build on one's knowledge? Temptation. Laziness. Ineffective teaching. Insufficient studying or time management. Lack of perspective—not seeing the big picture in their long-term development as artists. A prevailing lack of fundamental language instruction and knowledge of basic grammar (see Chapter 5). But also, curricular constraints, for if the instructor is not able to carry out this crucial element of best practice in diction

44 *From Imitation to Communication*

pedagogy, everything is set up to impede the singer's long-term development. Students leave the diction class with shortcomings, and in order to be prepared for opera workshop, coachings, or recitals, they immediately turn to outside resources as a quick shortcut. Along the way, they forget pronunciation rules. Since they have not developed critical skills in their study of outside resources, they fail to question what may be typographical errors or different approaches to pronunciation, and so must over-rely on coaches to correct their pronunciation. College language classes don't help with formal pronunciation because few instructors speak with formal pronunciation, and most of their classmates in the courses speak with inauthentic accents. College language courses in the United States don't delve into grammar until the second year of study.

Stage directors and coaches usually have no idea that the translations and IPA that students arrive with are not their own at all. Short-term gains may be impressive, but for the long-term, there are ramifications all down the line through graduate study, as we saw with my doctoral student, and into professional work.

Outside resources should be part of a huge array of useful tools that modern singers have at their disposal, but not substitutes for their own work. Let's look at some of these tools, most of them online, to see how best to utilize them, and how to shape a diction curriculum that sets students on an optimal path.

IPA: Pluses and Minuses

The IPA is a wonderful starting point for English-speaking singers. The adaptation of IPA for singing, simplifying the alphabet down to its most practical features, is extremely useful. By using an internationally recognized symbol to represent a sound, a singer is already one step away from falling into the habits of their own language. (Writing [e] instead of "ay," for example.) The abstract, universal symbol helps the brain to create a new area of sound formations.

In Cashman's research, lyric diction pedagogues cited the following as IPA's strengths[6]:

- It is international and uniform. This facilitates communication about lyric diction between professionals and students from different linguistic backgrounds.
- It is a means of transliteration that is abstracted from the singer's mother tongue.

From Imitation to Communication 45

- Its segmental approach is well suited to sung language. (The segmentation is also a pitfall, however, as shown below.)
- It allows students and professionals some degree of independence in their lyric diction work, allowing them to make use of outside resources. (This can also be a pitfall, however, if students completely rely on these resources.)

Cashman's interviewees cited the following aspects as IPA's weaknesses:

- It is not precise enough to reflect variations in sounds between languages and subtle variations of sounds within a language. (So, singers must learn the differences, for example, between [e] in the various languages.)
- It is ineffective without the singer having correctly learned the sound associated with each IPA symbol in each language context.[7]
- It represents language syllabically and is thus unable to represent aspects of prosody (suprasegmentals), "flow," and expression.
- An overemphasis on IPA may lead singers, and students in particular, to "sing IPA," and not to engage intellectually or emotionally with the language itself.

This last point is a very important one. Cashman continues:

Radcliffe said she finds that a focus on IPA leads to singers singing sounds rather than language. She explained: '[IPA] is symbols... It takes it away from the actual language element of it, and then you're just reading these signs rather than reading a language.' Kimmorley shared this perspective. She finds that singers who are reading an IPA transcription do not engage with the original language, and often lose sight of the words that led to the transcription.[8]

David Adams summarizes the pitfalls of IPA:

Valuable as IPA is, it is limited in the amount of information it can convey. This is particularly true of inflections over longer phrases. It also must be remembered that the IPA is a means to an end and not an end in itself. It is not uncommon to hear a singer who enunciates all sounds according to the 'rules' and yet sounds stilted and unidiomatic. One needs to get past the IPA to the language itself.[9]

46 *From Imitation to Communication*

Other than an introductory class, a diction course, then, must be substantial enough in scope that students are able to move past IPA into the language itself.[10] By the end of a diction class, students should be able to read a sentence in the original foreign language (with a translation provided, so they can read with understanding and intent), without IPA, and pronounce it fairly well. After all, that was one of the reasons for using the tool of IPA, to get to this point. Ironically, the most problematic language in this regard is Italian, in which IPA is the least useful tool! Italian often comes into play early in a singer's studies, and sometimes it is even used simultaneously as an introduction to IPA. Young singers tend to immediately consult the IPA in Nico Castel's Italian libretti books or IPA Source, write it into their scores, and read the IPA instead of the Italian. In doing so, they miss punctuation, the proper alignment of vowel clusters, and, especially in recitative, inflection. Their recitation by sight of a new Italian text is usually much worse than that of German or even French. Italians themselves simply use French accent marks in their Italian texts to show the quality of stressed *e*'s and *o*'s. Almost everything else is completely phonetic. This Italian diction dilemma will be discussed in Chapter 5. The point for now is that students must be taught to avoid the pitfall of using IPA as an end in itself; teachers must alter the perspective of many a young student that once they know IPA, they "know" diction. Cashman's interviewees agreed: "It is only a starting point for lyric diction learning, and must be perceived as such."[11]

Vocal Coachings

A private vocal coaching is also a tool for a singer. Singers need an extra, expert set of ears for feedback, suggestions, guidance, and insight into style, details of languages, and other matters. The best coachings occur when singers arrive with their best work, a specific goal, or a particular problem that they have been struggling with. A prevailing issue in music schools is that many singers arrive to regular coachings unprepared, not warmed up, with only a general idea of what they want to accomplish, or worse, the hope that the coach will teach them their music by rote. While some schools are able to provide regular coachings throughout many of their school years, some students fail to make the best use of them. The shock comes after they graduate and have to pay by the hour for a coaching. This issue with school coachings arises mainly from a lack of perspective, going hand in hand with curricular compartmentalization, treated in the next chapter. For now, the agreement of Cashman's interviewees provides

From Imitation to Communication 47

insight into how this problem can be addressed at the university level with regard to diction:

> Many noted the professional and financial advantages gained by professional singers when the lyric diction skills they have developed during conservatorium studies allow them to engage in thorough and independent preparation before seeking the input of a lyric diction coach.[12]

Self-Recordings after the Pandemic

One of the side effects of the pandemic that many of us have experienced has to do with students' increased critical listening skills, which is a main goal in diction classes. The process tended to go like this:

1 Students submitted a recording for an opera/opera workshop project, for feedback.
2 Feedback was given. The students worked on the issues and sent another recording.
3 Feedback was given. The students worked on the issues and sent another recording.
4 Feedback was given—"Did you really not hear that you left out that double consonant?" The students worked on the issues and sent another recording.
5 At some point, the student began to listen much more critically before sending another recording, realizing they could have saved themselves a lot of work and time by listening more critically in the first place. New projects and new repertoire were then met with better preparation. Many students cited this improvement in their listening skills as a source that propelled themselves toward greater independence. This is certainly something we must continue to foster! It is also a sign that our voice curricula have tended to foster dependence instead of independence. Coachings were one way of substituting for much of a student's own work.

Yet, students and professionals have been recording themselves for decades. Student singers have regularly recorded their voice lessons, private coachings, and rehearsals and listened back in their car, apartment, dorm, or practice room. What changed during the pandemic? Perhaps it is that most of their pandemic recordings involved actual performances, so that their listening covered all aspects of their performance, instead of focusing on just one element—students learned

48 *From Imitation to Communication*

to listen better to both details and the whole. Above all, though, it can be attributed to the fact that students were isolated, not hurrying from class to class, allowing them more time to reflect and focus. This time for regular self-reflection and self-evaluation, too, should be built in to our approaches. Artists need this, and so do developing artists! This is in line with the recommendation of Angela Myles Beeching, leading consultant/author on career preparation for musicians, and former Director of the Center for Entrepreneurship at Manhattan School of Music. Even before the pandemic, Beeching wrote that at least one hour a week, it is critically important for students to "unplug [from technology], and go by themselves somewhere in nature to reflect; to process."[13]

YouTube

YouTube first appeared in 2005. According to extensive research by Corey Seemiller and Meghan Grace, almost 90% of all Generation Z college students go to YouTube to acquire new knowledge.[14] For college voice students, the amount is probably closer to 100%—instant access to YouTube and its enormous wealth of performances makes it an immediate go-to tool for students learning new repertoire.

Before the invention of YouTube, we always cautioned students to listen to at least several commercial recordings, as listening to just one would lead to copying. With YouTube, however, anyone can post a recording, and many are sub-par. Writing in 2011, Scott McCoy pointed out that "As teachers, we have a huge responsibility to help our students filter this material."[15] Robert Marks summarized the situation well when he wrote in 2013: "Unfortunately, the online world of YouTube has become a mixed blessing."[16]

The negative effects of learning from YouTube have led to some creative pedagogical approaches. For example, Semyon Rozin intentionally designed his summer programs in Vianden, Luxembourg and Saarburg, Germany so that students study and perform only music that has never been recorded. This has resulted in some wonderful (re)discoveries of works by lesser known composers and has forced students to learn music based solely on the score and their knowledge of musical styles. Although extremely valuable and enlightening, this approach is hardly practical for a student singer's regular routine.

For those singers who have relied on YouTube to learn their music, sight-singing tests incorporated into auditions can reveal deficiencies in their abilities. Deficiencies are addressed in sight-singing and ear training classes and followed up in voice juries before the singers are allowed to continue to the next level.

From Imitation to Communication 49

For diction, by taking McCoy's admonition to heart, YouTube has become a valuable tool for comparative listening and the development of critical listening skills. Since the whole gamut is there— great artists with great diction, great artists with different approaches, artists affected by regionalisms, well-known artists with bad diction, or unknown artists worthy of our discovery—pertinent examples can easily be presented in a diction class, and comparative listening assignments can be made, as well. This builds on the work of some teachers before the dawn of YouTube[17] and helps guide students in the best use of YouTube as the amazing tool it can be.

Nico Castel's Opera Libretti

I remember teaching an Italian diction class in the 1990s. Nico Castel's volumes of Italian libretti with word-for-word translations and IPA had just begun to appear.[18] When I mentioned these to my students as very useful resources, a palpable silence came over the class, as if these books were taboo, a form of cheating. One undergraduate raised her hand and said, "I prefer to look up each word myself. That way I can see all the different shades of meaning, and make my own personal choice. My Italian also gets better that way."

Over time, however, younger students began to lose the perspective of the student who had raised her hand. It became apparent how valuable the books, and the many volumes to follow, were, especially for Castel's translations and informative footnotes commenting on historical and cultural context, and often archaic idioms. For advanced singers, they became an extra tool. When notified that they had been given an opera role, students immediately wrote Castel's (controversial) Italian IPA into their scores. They tended to read from the IPA instead of from the Italian text, even though Italian is mostly phonetic. This created added problems with inflection and lining up triphthongs and double diphthongs. Because the translation was an added outside element, as well, they had to work harder to connect with their text. Some singers did not even know the meaning of some of the English words Castel had chosen and did not look up those words, either. Issues were eventually sorted out in coachings, but the process that Radcliffe had described as crucial for high quality diction had been side-stepped, and a bad habit had begun.

Famed soprano Beverly Sills summed up the value of Castel's resources well when she wrote "His work can be the finishing touch for many a singer."[19] For students, the question is how to make these books the finishing touch, and not the first step.

50 *From Imitation to Communication*

Just as YouTube can be utilized in a diction class, with students learning how to use YouTube critically, Castel's work should also be introduced into a diction class. My approach is to have students work in small groups with an excerpt from an opera. I provide them with a few pages of music and translations and ask them to figure out the IPA. Then, I write on the board what they came up with, one word at a time, listen to them pronounce it, and we discuss rules and phrasal doublings as we go. Finally, I hand them Castel's IPA version and we compare that with what they had come up with. Since Castel modified some Italian vowels based on what he thought was optimal for a typical singer, there will be plenty of differences to discuss. Students learn that they should put in the time of doing their own IPA first and make comparisons afterward. Castel's approach for Italian may not align with their individual voices. They also see that Castel almost never shows phrasal doublings, leaving that to the singer. So, students learn to look up phrasal doublings, too, and not wait for coaches to tell them where they are. As for translations, this is discussed below, under "Online Dictionaries and Translators."

IPA Source

In 2003, Bard Suverkrop launched IPA Source, an online resource (www.ipasource.com) with word-for-word English translations, idiomatic translations, and IPA for thousands of individual songs and arias in six languages, with more languages planned. Over 50% of the site's material is unique to IPA Source.

Many schools subscribe to IPA Source, making it available to students for free. Whereas Castel's books are hard copies, IPA Source is accessible to a student with a click of a mouse. Like YouTube, IPA Source needs to be introduced into a diction course in such a way that students learn to use it as a valuable supplementary tool, and not as a habitual replacement for their own work. Colleagues and I saw students' use of IPA Source as a replacement for their own work appear gradually over time, and by more and more students. The handwriting of their song texts was the students', but the translations and some of the IPA symbols, as well as the occasional typo, were clearly recognizable as coming verbatim from IPA Source (which can be plagiarism, depending on the assignment!). Some students would simply print pages from IPA Source and hand them in! The pitfall here is for diction classes to become a way of learning IPA simply for the purpose of being able to look up Nico Castel and IPA Source for their pronunciation, like the doctoral student who had fallen into this trap. Very soon

From Imitation to Communication 51

they forget how to do the work themselves, and only progress so far in their careers. The temptation can come from poor time management, or by trying to assure themselves a good grade. Seemiller and Grace assert with significant research that Generation Z students are predisposed to using digital resources for "accessing a quick answer to complete an assignment," and for skipping steps that are seen as too time-consuming.[20] Short-term results in undergraduate studies can be quite impressive, but they come at the expense of accomplishing much more important long-term goals. An approach to introducing IPA Source is included in the following discussion.

Online Dictionaries and Translators

When learning a new song, many students will first turn to YouTube, followed by IPA Source for translations and IPA. In my classes, I stress that the first step when learning a new song is not to consult either of these sources, but to write down a translation of each individual word beneath each foreign word—a word-for-word translation—and from there make an idiomatic translation. They need to know the meaning of each word if they are to connect with the text emotionally and intellectually. So, this is always the first step. It will tell them where the most important, expressive words are. Jumping immediately into pronunciation means that students are making sounds with no meaning. Or, they are simply following rules and writing down IPA without even thinking about the sounds. Even if they have had little or no study of the language, they can look up individual words. In this way, students are able to choose shades of meaning that resonate with them, and learn how to translate: both resulting in a more intimate understanding of the language. This is the beginning of the disciplined commitment to text for which Radcliffe and diction pedagogues worldwide advocate.

Translations can come from hardback dictionaries, or from online sources, such as www.WordReference.com or www.reverso.net. When using online translators, I stress to students not to input entire phrases at first, but only single words. Putting in entire phrases will usually not tell them the meaning of individual words. Inserting single words reveals a plethora of meanings from which they can choose. After searching individual words, students can then make an idiomatic translation or submit entire phrases into the online resource to compare their translation with the online one. Knowing the entire meaning of a phrase can also help with the meaning of any individual words they had problems with. I make it clear that I do not grade

52   *From Imitation to Communication*

translations, since this is not a language class, but I can easily tell how much effort they put into it. If they are completely stumped, they can leave that word blank and I will help them. I will later give written corrections and suggestions for their translations. Common suggestions are:

1   If the word-for-word translation makes sense, then leave it alone. This will help your memory if the word order is the same in both languages. It also makes a good translation for recital supertitles, as the audience will hear expressive words in the same order as the translation.
2   If you have a cognate, it is usually good to use it. For example, if you see *tranquilla*, why write *peaceful* when you can put *tranquil*? It is good for your memory and will help the audience, too, when they see the translation.

For some students, this is all entirely new. For those who have been relying completely on IPA Source, this will get them back on track. For those who already have a good feel for the language, this process sets them up for the other main singing languages they are not yet familiar with.

When they understand the text, then they can put in their IPA above each word. After they have written their IPA, *now* is the time for them to turn to IPA Source as a check on their IPA work and compare their translations. Of course, we will have already looked at IPA Source in class to see how text and IPA were presented there, what symbols might have been different from what they were used to, and why, and have noted any typographical errors that might have occurred.

I also recommend IPA Source as an excellent tool for self-study and review. Students select a text they are not familiar with from their collections of music, complete their IPA, and then go to IPA Source to check their work. If there are discrepancies, they can figure out what they did wrong or email me with questions.

I had one industrious first-year student recently who, when handing in his work, went as far as showing the symbols he had changed after looking at IPA Source. He also pointed out a typographical error in IPA Source's version. I had already been impressed with his expressive singing, and his enthusiastic and insightful comments in class. This student had no extraordinary background in languages, but he was well on his way for placing text study high on his priority list and laying a solid foundation of using outside resources critically to his best advantage.

The Diction Police

This site, www.dictionpolice.com, was launched by François Germain and Ellen Rissinger in 2010. The approach is different from IPA Source, in that the main emphasis is on hearing sounds and texts delivered by native speakers who are singers or coaches well-versed in the formal rules of lyric diction. This is an excellent supplemental resource, then. The site also includes hundreds of texts with IPA and translations for several languages, video tutorials and review courses, and it offers podcasts and webinars. It is available for reasonably priced individual and studio subscriptions. So, in terms of incorporating The Diction Police into a diction class, it might be possible to obtain school funding to purchase a studio subscription.

DictionBuddy

Launched in 2019 by Kofi Hayford, Viktoriya Koreneva, and Emma Lavandier, www.dictionbuddy.com, DictionBuddy—"Created by singers for singers in the 21st Century"—is an exciting new addition to diction help for singers. Like IPA Source, this online resource is available by paid subscription, either individually, by voice studio, or by academic institution, and is very affordable. Designed for use on a tablet or smartphone, DictionBuddy consists of a downloadable app that features native speakers, who are also professional singers, speaking texts in nine languages, both naturally and at a very slow tempo, while the screen shows the original text, word-for-word translations, idiomatic translations, and IPA. (Translations and IPA are provided mostly by Cheri Montgomery.)

DictionBuddy wisely cautions that the app is not an end in itself but should be used along with other resources and under the guidance of students' teachers and coaches. Just what that guidance should consist of, they don't say. I would suggest that it should be introduced and incorporated into a diction class similarly to Castel's opera libretti books, YouTube, and IPA Source. Namely, not as an immediate go-to resource that would lead to mimicking, but *after* a student's own in-depth study of the text, for refinement. However, it is certainly good at the very beginning of a student's training to just get a feel for the sound and flow of the language. For critical listening, it is important to note that the Italian speakers hardly use phrasal doublings at all, even though in the 21st century phrasal doublings are much more of a consistent formal standard for lyric diction in Italy than in previous decades. It is also interesting to compare a native speaker-singer's

54 *From Imitation to Communication*

natural delivery of the text with the slow one. The normal delivery, though very clear, does not always adhere to formal rules in detail, while the slow one does. This is educational in and of itself and important for students to be able to hear. As with The Diction Police, hearing a native speaker's overall sound and natural inflection and homing in on individual sounds are great tools.

Language Tools

There are now many self-paced language programs enhanced by 21st-century technology, involving interactive software or websites, digital downloads, mobile apps, and/or live virtual exchange. Most notably are Rosetta Stone, Babel, Rocket Languages, Pimsleur, and Glossika. Although they do not provide course credit, they are great for furthering one's language study, or keeping up one's skills. As time and money are ever-present considerations, Duolingo, whose website and mobile app are free, is an excellent alternative for keeping up one's language skills in as little as ten minutes a day. Used wisely—by repeating phrases out loud with perfect pronunciation, and by concentrated, focused listening—the free, fun-to-use tool is practically a no-brainer for advancing one's skills with the least amount of financial and time commitment.

Digital Memory Tools

American bass-baritone Mark S. Doss is a wonderful example of a thriving artist who, after singing 100 roles with more than 60 major opera houses around the world, continues to passionately explore new ways of learning and connecting with text. Some of these approaches are physical, involving jumping rope, juggling, lifting light weights (!), and tossing scarves, all while declaiming text from memory and connecting with emotionally packed words. Others are digital, such as the use of flashcard programs like iFlash[21] and Anki.[22] These technologies allow the user to embed images, audio, and video onto a digital card; to search a word to see where it occurs throughout a poem or entire opera role; and to take advantage of spaced repetition, a proven method by cognitive scientists for speeding long-term memory.[23] Doss uses these programs not only for the original foreign text, but also for testing his memory of the translation:

> I have used iFlash very effectively, which gives instant feedback for SPEAKING the phrases of the text and having them play back

From Imitation to Communication 55

in a timed mode. Anki is also a very good program for the same thing, but it also allows you to TYPE out the answer (translation) to a phrase, which is a good muscle memory tool.[24]

The importance of writing out one's text to help with memory, both digitally and by hand, will be taken up again in Chapter 5.

Yet another helpful digital memory tool is available at Productivity501.[25] After text is typed or pasted into the tool's box, the text is shown in another box with only the first letter of each word, but with all the original punctuation and any capitalized letters. This method puts text into short-term memory as quickly as possible, where it can then be recalled instead of merely repeated, thus strengthening long-term memory.

Virtual Exchange

Virtual exchange—in which students collaborate with foreign peers one-on-one independently—is one of the most important educational innovations of the 21st century to date. Not only does this technological tool provide the ability to enhance essential diction skills, but it also gives a ready answer to the question *How can DEI and 21st-century elements be assimilated* within *a diction class?* Virtual exchange is fully explored in Chapter 6.

As with quite a few 21st-century classes across many fields, best practice in diction pedagogy involves guiding students in the best use of digital resources. This guidance is critical and is a further argument against reducing the number of hours allotted to diction instruction.

Notes

1. Malcolm Gladwell, *Outliers: The Story of Success* (New York: Back Bay Books, 2008), 35–38.
2. Milan Kundera, *Testaments Betrayed: An Essay in Nine Parts*, trans. from the French by Linda Asher (New York: HarperCollins, 1995), 135.
3. Penelope Cashman, "International Best Practice in the Teaching of Lyric Diction to Conservatorium-Level Singers" (PhD diss., Elder Conservatorium of Music, University of Adelaide, 2019), 212. Available at https://digital.library.adelaide.edu.au/dspace/handle/2440/120990.
4. Ibid., p. 191.
5. Mark Rabideau places tenacity with curiosity, creativity, and collaboration as key to creating a musician's career, in his *Creating the Revolutionary Artist: Entrepreneurship for the 21st-Century Musician* (Lanham, MD: Rowman & Littlefield, 2018), 14.

56 *From Imitation to Communication*

6. Cashman, "International Best Practice in the Teaching of Lyric Diction to Conservatorium-Level Singers," 230–231.
7. Frequently, singers with no knowledge of Czech simply ask me for the IPA, not realizing that they must know what the symbols mean specifically for Czech! Listening to a recording will give them an idea, but will not go far enough.
8. Cashman, "International Best Practice in the Teaching of Lyric Diction to Conservatorium-Level Singers," 236.
9. David Adams, *A Handbook of Diction for Singers: Italian, German, French*. 2nd ed. (New York: Oxford University Press, 2008), xii–xiii.
10. An introductory IPA class is sometimes called "Phonics." The format is usually one hour a week, and IPA symbols are shown comparatively, for example, showing [e] with examples of where this sound would occur in English, Italian, German, and French, and how the symbol can represent different shades of sound. First-year students learn the basics of IPA and receive a basic overview of the languages they will be communicating in. This is an excellent way for entering first-year students to begin their lyric diction studies.
11. Cashman, "International Best Practice in the Teaching of Lyric Diction to Conservatorium-Level Singers," 236.
12. Ibid., p. 191.
13. Michael Stepniak, and Peter Sirotin, *Beyond the Conservatory Model: Reimagining Classical Music Performance Training in Higher Education. CMS Emerging Fields in Music* (New York: Routledge, 2020), 42–43. Members of Generation Z also recognize the need for them to step back from technology now and then. See Corey Seemiller and Meghan Grace, *Generation Z: A Century in the Making* (New York: Routledge, 2019), 50.
14. Seemiller and Grace, *Generation Z*, 207.
15. Scott McCoy, "Pedagogic Truth in the Age of YouTube," *Journal of Singing: The Official Journal of the National Association of Teachers of Singing* 67, no. 5 (May/June 2011): 550.
16. Robert Marks, "I Learned it from YouTube! (And Other Challenges of Teaching Voice)," *Journal of Singing: The Official Journal of the National Association of Teachers of Singing*, 69, no. 5 (May/June 2013): 591.
17. For example: Andrew Adams, "Unstressed E's and O's in Italian Lyric Diction: A Comparison of Diction Texts," *Journal of Singing: The Official Journal of the National Association of Teachers of Singing* 59, no. 4 (March/April 2003): 337–338.
18. Beginning with *The Complete Puccini Libretti in Two Volumes* (New York: Leyerle Publications, 1993 & 1994).
19. Beverly Sills, foreword to Nico Castel, *French Opera Libretti in Two Volumes, Vol. I* (Mt. Morris, NY: Leyerle Publications, 1999): xiii.
20. Seemiller and Grace, *Generation Z*, 203, 236.
21. Designed for Apple products, available at http://www.loopware.com/iflash/.
22. "Anki" is Japanese for "memorization." Available at https://apps.ankiweb.net.
23. This is the basis of the Duolingo language-learning program. See "Spaced Repetition," *Wikipedia*, accessed June 2, 2021, https://en.wikipedia.org/wiki/Spaced_repetition.

From Imitation to Communication   57

24. Email to the author, May 31, 2021. Used with permission.
25. Mark Shead, "How to Memorize Verbatim Text," *Productivity501*, accessed June 2, 2021, http://www.productivity501.com/how-to-memorize-verbatim-text/294/. Other resources are given by Mark Shead at "How to Memorize Resources," *Productivity501*, accessed June 2, 2021, http://www.productivity501.com/how-to-memorize/714/.

Bibliography

Adams, Andrew. "Unstressed E's and O's in Italian Lyric Diction: A Comparison of Diction Texts." *Journal of Singing: The Official Journal of the National Association of Teachers of Singing* 59, no. 4 (March/April 2003): 333–339.

Adams, David. *A Handbook of Diction for Singers: Italian, German, French*. 2nd ed. New York: Oxford University Press, 2008.

Cashman, Penelope. "International Best Practice in the Teaching of Lyric Diction to Conservatorium-Level Singers." PhD diss., Elder Conservatorium of Music, University of Adelaide, 2019. Available at https://digital.library.adelaide.edu.au/dspace/handle/2440/120990.

Castel, Nico. *The Complete Puccini Libretti in Two Volumes*. New York: Leyerle Publications, 1993 & 1994.

Gladwell, Malcolm. *Outliers: The Story of Success*. New York: Back Bay Books, 2008.

Kundera, Milan. *Testaments Betrayed: An Essay in Nine Parts*, trans. from the French by Linda Asher. New York: HarperCollins, 1995.

Marks, Robert. "I Learned It from YouTube! (And Other Challenges of Teaching Voice)." *Journal of Singing: The Official Journal of the National Association of Teachers of Singing* 69, no. 5 (May/June 2013): 589–592.

McCoy, Scott. "Pedagogic Truth in the Age of YouTube." *Journal of Singing: The Official Journal of the National Association of Teachers of Singing* 67, no. 5 (May/June 2011): 549–550.

Rabideau, Mark. *Creating the Revolutionary Artist: Entrepreneurship for the 21st-Century Musician*. Lanham, MD: Rowman & Littlefield, 2018.

Seemiller, Corey, and Meghan Grace. *Generation Z: A Century in the Making*. New York: Routledge, 2019.

Shead, Mark. "How to Memorize Resources." *Productivity501*. Accessed June 2, 2021. http://www.productivity501.com/how-to-memorize/714/.

——————. "How to Memorize Verbatim Text." *Productivity501*. Accessed June 2, 2021. http://www.productivity501.com/how-to-memorize-verbatim-text/294/.

Sills, Beverly. Foreword to Castel, Nico. *French Opera Libretti in Two Volumes, Vol. I*. Mt. Morris, NY: Leyerle Publications, 1999.

Stepniak, Michael, with Peter Sirotin. *Beyond the Conservatory Model: Reimagining Classical Music Performance Training in Higher Education. CMS Emerging Fields in Music*. New York: Routledge, 2020.

Wikipedia. "Spaced Repetition." Accessed June 2, 2021. https://en.wikipedia.org/wiki/Spaced_repetition.

5 From Compartmentalization to Transformation

Meeting New Challenges for Today's Singers

> For me, diction IS technique. Or at least a fundamental part of it!
>
> I always look at it as part of an artistic whole, and am always thinking how the tools of diction can serve as a springboard into the emotional and dramatic meat of the material that moves us to tears, joy, and laughter.
>
> (Nicholas Phan, renowned tenor)[1]

Once we identify new challenges for incoming students, how can we best address them? Then, how can we avoid compartmentalization and siloing? How can we best foster independence?

There are really two issues here, two pitfalls:

1 Not coming to terms with our era's particularly inadequate pre-college foreign language study in English-speaking countries, as well as students' lack of knowledge of English grammar in the United States, and how that affects diction instruction, curricula, and just about everything else in a voice student's studies; and, when this is not addressed head-on:

2 Not being able to give students the tools, perspective, and motivation they need to dedicate themselves to a passionate, lifelong exploration of diction, language, and text beyond their required courses.

This chapter focuses on students' first two years of undergraduate study. It posits that the first year—a *foundational* year—is inherently compartmentalized and siloed and examines what that means for laying a foundation for short-term and long-term success in diction classes. It also argues that beginning with the sophomore year—a *transformational* year—it is possible to break free of compartmentalization and

DOI: 10.4324/9781003226208-6

From Compartmentalization to Transformation 59

siloing and set students on a path of success fueled by curiosity, collaboration, and perspective. Once the first year has laid a good foundation, the transformational second year helps make the integration of singers' skills much easier for everyone. The second year, too, is ripe for students' focused exploration, in which a virtual exchange can begin.

The First-Year Student: Avoiding Deficit Teaching

By looking at short-term vs. long-term development, pitfalls to avoid, and the strengths and needs of incoming first-year students, I contend that the *worst* semester to schedule a foreign language diction class is a student's very first semester. When colleagues at other institutions contact me to ask about diction curricula, this is usually the issue—what may have worked in the past does not work now, and some schools are operating with curricula put into place decades ago. The exception is an introductory IPA class. An English diction course also works well here, or a combination of both. The IPA class lays an immediate foundation for students' work. English is spoken by everyone in the class, so detailed work can begin immediately in an English diction class. Incoming first-year students are joined together socially, as a siloed group that works well in this case, and can sing for one another in a supportive environment. Foreign language diction can then begin the second semester if necessary, but the sophomore year—which can be truly transformative—is optimal.

Many schools already operate this way, but need to still be aware of the issues, because they affect a singer's development throughout their studies and beyond. Some schools, however, are struggling with making a first-year Italian diction class work or are contemplating moving their diction classes to the first year as a way to better prepare their students, when, in fact, this would only make their situation worse.

What are the needs of this era's incoming first-year voice students? What does it mean to lay a solid foundation that first year?

Foreign Language Study

Voice majors are required to attain at least a basic working knowledge of the three main singing languages: Italian, German, and French. As we have seen, those who go beyond this, by developing a lifelong passion for languages, are the most successful communicators, the most successful and interesting singers. As established in Chapter 2, helping to spark this passion is an important part of best practice in diction

60 *From Compartmentalization to Transformation*

pedagogy. This passion, too, taps into a student's innate curiosity, and knowledge of foreign languages opens doors to international collaboration, relationships, and cultural exchange. Also, a singer's profession usually involves collaborating with musicians from all over the world. Singers can easily find themselves in the midst of a rehearsal where everyone is speaking Italian, German, or French. No, no one can expect an English-speaking singer to learn three foreign languages fluently, nor is that necessary, but a basic knowledge of each is fundamental, and advanced abilities in one of the three is desirable (or even fluency in *any* other language), as learning one foreign language teaches the brain how to approach other languages.[2]

In 1999, famed American soprano Beverly Sills wrote:

> I think that few would dispute that in general the American singer of today is the best trained in the world. The only aspect in which he or she might be at a disadvantage is in the matter of pronunciation. Actually it is more than mere pronunciation. It is in the freedom and imagination with which a singer can play around with the words that true and individual artistry is projected.[3]

Sills was multilingual since childhood, but for most English-speaking singers acquisition of foreign language skills has always been difficult. Let's fast-forward to 2021, in which the situation is arguably worse.

An 18-year-old American first-year student may, perhaps, enter college with a fairly strong skill in one foreign language, *if* the student studied the language for four years in high school. Some entering students may even be bilingual.[4] There is plenty of data, however, to show that *most* will enter with little foreign language skills. Some talented singers will have none at all.[5] In the United States, there is no national requirement to study a foreign language, so what is taught, when, and the quality, vary from state to state. In 47 states, there is no requirement at all for homeschoolers to study a foreign language. According to a 2017 report by the American Councils for International Education, only 20% of K–12 students studied a foreign language. Contrast that with Europeans, where there are national requirements, and the median is 92%. (100% of French children study a foreign language.) Most European children, too, begin foreign language study between the ages of 6 and 9 and continue for nine years, whereas most of the American children who do study a foreign language begin in middle or high school and stop after one or two years.[6] The ACTFL (American Council on the Teaching of Foreign Languages) does much to promote language education in the United

States, and there are wonderful teachers across the country, but the two years of foreign language that many top universities require—or only recommend—of incoming undergraduates is a bare minimum. Some renowned institutions that include prominent music departments surprisingly require no foreign language study at all of their entering students.[7]

For a profession in which diction standards have never been higher and at least a minimum basic knowledge of *three* foreign languages is required, it is startling that most American singers begin college with little foreign language skills! And depending on the college students attend, some gain no foreign language acquisition at all. It is not necessary to be able to speak a foreign language in order to convincingly sing in it, but having little to no exposure to *any* foreign language makes for a steep learning curve in forming foreign sounds, and then moving past the singing of segmented foreign sounds to expressive communication. Of course, this lack of foreign language study is one reason that IPA for singers caught on in English-speaking countries much more than elsewhere, but diction standards are higher now than at any other time for a professional singer. While this low level of language study increases the challenges of teaching a foreign language diction class to incoming students, this is not the only issue. When we add the lack of American students' English grammar knowledge on top of this, plus the compartmentalization and siloing of students' study, we arrive at the reason for the challenges of carrying out best practice in diction pedagogy. All of which points to ramifications all down the line.

English Grammar

Let's define grammar as not only grammar terminology, but spelling, punctuation, capitalization, and usage. For many of us, students' lack of grammar caught us by surprise, as its effects were gradual over the years. Now, however, we are all—in almost every field—very much aware of the challenges this poses, but it is especially challenging for teachers of diction, acting, and foreign languages.

We can take nothing for granted. We cannot assume that a student knows what "infinitive" means, or even "noun," let alone "3rd-person plural." We even have to make clear the difference between a "phrase" and a "sentence." A colleague stage director was wondering why he received blank stares when he said he needed more modifiers, more adjectives, and adverbs. But let's go to even more basic uses of grammar.

62 *From Compartmentalization to Transformation*

These are not exaggerations.[8] In a diction class of first-year students, and many a sophomore, it is now to be expected that:

- Many students copy a song text and leave out all punctuation, even if they are told emphatically to be attentive to it because punctuation is an actor's best friend, more fundamental than IPA.
- Many students leave out all capitalization, even if they are shown how helpful it is that German nouns are always capitalized, and that nouns are usually expressive words they need to connect with emotionally.
- Many students make frequent spelling errors, which means that their IPA and pronunciation are wrong for those words.
- Many students think in short phrases. This was first pointed out to me by a drama faculty colleague. Thinking in long phrases has always been a challenge, but now it is much more so.

There are two reasons for these issues. One involves technology, especially texting (short phrases, no punctuation or capitalization) and ingrained methods of note-taking. Spelling errors come from relying on spell check, which is not available when writing by hand. If writing on a computer, errors come from not always realizing that spell check is changing the spelling of some of the foreign words. Spell check can also change capitalization. Spell check and the students' changing of file formats can also alter digital IPA symbols.

Lack of grammar in the United States, however, mainly comes from changes in pedagogical approaches to English writing classes. Findings from dozens of studies over the last decades have shown that isolated grammar instruction is apparently of absolutely no help in the development of writing skills and can actually be detrimental.[9] As a result of this research, grammar is now taught in context, through the process of writing, and that process is not completed with the senior year of high school.

In 2017, Dana Goldstein reported for the *New York Times* that, despite (or because of?) changes introduced by the Common Core State Standards Initiative in the USA in 2010, "Students continue to arrive on college campuses needing remediation in basic writing skills."[10] The latest results, in 2018, of the Program for International Student Assessment (PISA), which tests 15-year-olds worldwide in reading, math, and science, found "no significant improvement or decline" in reading among American 15-year-olds since 2000, the year PISA began their tests.[11] In 2019, Goldstein returned to report about these PITA results in the *New York Times*, saying "There is no

From Compartmentalization to Transformation 63

consensus on why the performance of struggling students is declining. Education experts argue vociferously about a range of potential causes, including... *a dearth of instruction in basic skills like phonics.*"[12] (The italics are my own.) Her article concludes by saying that experts are still hopeful that with renewed efforts, students will improve, mainly citing the need for better teacher training. With this attitude, plus the evidence about the futility of isolated grammar instruction, this means that grammar errors and lack of grammar knowledge are not going away! While the pedagogical approach may be beneficial in making Americans better writers in the long run (but apparently not better readers), it is obviously not geared toward someone whose profession will involve rewriting, translating, and communicating formal texts in several languages. It has, then, definitely made the education of American singers and collaborative pianists more difficult. At least drama students deal only with English, and foreign language teachers can continue to teach grammar in context.[13] To try to make up for these unanticipated problems, students and some diction teachers have turned outside resources like IPA Source into life preservers, when such resources should have acted as excellent supplemental resources (see Chapter 4).

In diction classes, we are not asking students to create new texts. We do, or should, ask them to translate to the best of their abilities, but the foreign texts are already written. The key to communicating those texts lies in knowing the meaning of the words, the rules of their pronunciation, and forming the correct sounds. From there we learn how to connect the words and decide which words are inflected and how to bring them out, all of which necessitates knowing where a sentence begins and ends, where the dependent clauses are, what a comma does for meaning, or why there is an ellipsis, and how we keep in L2 (second language) diction mode in the midst of heated emotional moments on the stage. It requires laying the foundation for the kind of dedicated text work we saw in a thriving professional such as Mark S. Doss, in Chapter 4, or such as tenor Nicholas Phan, whose quote is at the head of this chapter, or just about any famous singer that comes to mind. Diction is interwoven with everything a singer does. For all these reasons, diction classes cannot be watered down or separated from a necessary holistic approach.

I do not think that we need to use many grammar terms in order to teach lyric diction well, but there is a minimum amount of terminology we do need in order to effectively and efficiently teach. For example, I have to use the words "infinitive" and "conjugation" in Italian diction to talk about stress, how to look up words in a dictionary,

64   *From Compartmentalization to Transformation*

and the pronunciation of stressed *e*'s and *o*'s. Identifying "3rd-person plural" in French tells us how to pronounce the final vowel; in Italian, it tells us that the stress is not on the penultimate syllable, where we would otherwise expect it.

While text work for singers can, and should, be covered in other classes, text work cannot, and must not, be erased from diction classes. (Other than perhaps an introductory IPA course.) That would lead to mindless sounds and complete dependence on outside resources and coaches to make sense of the sounds. In other words, compartmentalization, lack of integration, and "worst practice" instead of best practice as defined by leading diction pedagogues in Chapter 2. This is not a matter of duplicating material that might be covered elsewhere in an acting class, coaching, or voice lesson. It is a matter of approaching text work as a common, unifying element in voice students' work. This is integration and overlapping, working as a team of educators, with each member of the team reinforcing one another's text work and approaching it from different angles. Now, more than ever, work on text *must* be the common denominator in *all* aspects of students' vocal studies—diction classes, voice lessons, coachings, vocal literature, and opera workshop.

How do we avoid deficit teaching for undergraduate voice majors? By recognizing that students are certainly no less intelligent, and that the elimination of dry grammar exercises from school curricula has meant that students are now more creative writers, and they become better writers in the long run. That doesn't solve the issue, though— we also avoid deficit teaching in diction classes by finding a way to teach what is needed to lay a solid foundation for independence, *and* by adjusting our curricula, if necessary, to allow for this kind of teaching. We do not deal with it by trying to do what we have always done, or throwing up our hands and telling students to just imitate what they hear, and use someone else's IPA and translations all the time. It is a huge adjustment for a typical first-year student to confront the detailed aspects of foreign sounds, foreign text, and IPA in today's world, when the differences between a written [i], [ɪ], and [I] seem inconsequential. The first year, then, should take advantage of inherently compartmentalized classes and lay a foundation that enables transformative diction classes the following years.[14]

I am happy to teach the minimum amount of grammar terminology needed to help singers on their path to expressive communication.[15] The problem at the first-year level is the amount of time it takes for some students to learn to copy a written foreign text correctly, and to pay attention to punctuation—weeks for some, months for others.

From Compartmentalization to Transformation 65

If it's not correct, some of the sounds will be completely wrong, or they will miss the meaning behind their sounds. Why should we insist that students write out their texts, then, if this is such an issue? Why not just copy and paste it, or download it, and be done with it? In 2017, Goldstein states about writing:

> There is a notable shortage of high-quality research on the teaching of writing, but studies that do exist point toward a few concrete strategies that help students perform better on writing tests. First, children need to learn how to transcribe both by hand and through typing on a computer. Teachers report that many students who can produce reams of text on their cellphones are unable to work effectively at a laptop, desktop, or even in a paper notebook because they've become so anchored to the small mobile screen. Quick communication on a smartphone almost requires writers to eschew rules of grammar and punctuation, exactly the opposite of what is wanted on the page.[16]

As a concrete diction example, Thomas Grubb in his wonderful exercises in *Singing in French* asks the reader to first copy the given French song and aria texts, underline the vowels that are underlined in the book, and then write the IPA for the corresponding underlined vowels.[17] For the first time in 28 years, a student from my class complained about the necessity of copying the text. It was a waste of time, she said. She wanted to be handed a PDF of the text and simply add her IPA. She failed to see the value of physically reproducing French spelling and punctuation as one way to meticulously and methodically learn how French spelling, with all of its accent marks and circumflexes, works. She wanted a shortcut to the learning process, and even typing in the text was not short enough. This example is completely in line with the findings of Seemiller and Grace, in which Generation Z students prefer to skip steps they see as too time-consuming.[18]

Another value of copying text is for memorization, as we saw in Chapter 4. This has been used by professional singers for centuries, of course, but research from the last few years affirms the value of writing out text *by hand* as a valuable tool for improving memory. The results of a 2020 study conducted in Norway, detail findings that are especially pertinent for singers:

> The results were quite clear. Both adolescent and adult brains are much more active while writing in comparison to typing. 'The use of pen and paper gives the brain more "hooks" to hang your

66 *From Compartmentalization to Transformation*

memories on. Writing by hand creates much more activity in the sensorimotor parts of the brain. A lot of senses are activated by pressing the pen on paper, seeing the letters you write and hearing the sound you make while writing. These sense experiences create contact between different parts of the brain and open the brain up for learning. We both learn better and remember better,' Professor Audrey van der Meer explains in a media release.[19]

Punctuation for a singing actor is as fundamental a tool as IPA is. Integrating this simple but powerful tool into a diction class is crucial for inflection and communication. The bulk of best practice diction time, however, should be spent on learning sounds, IPA, rules, and communication—and now, best use of technology—and when it takes weeks of reminders and mini-presentations for first-year students and some sophomores to finally learn to copy a foreign text correctly, and to also provide the correct punctuation and capitalization in their English translations, the issue must be addressed.

The lack of grammar and foreign language study has ramifications down the road, too. University foreign language instructors tell me that they cannot cover as much material as they used to.[20] Esteemed Professor of Collaborative Piano Martin Katz, while maintaining his extensive translation and diction requirements for his doctoral students at the University of Michigan, has had to drop one of the three language translation requirements for his Master's students and Specialist (Artist Diploma) students:

> I held out for a very long time against reducing the M.M. rules, but more than half of the very intelligent students simply had no background in grammar IN ENGLISH and thus found it very difficult to understand conjugation, declension, etc. The foreign students from Europe and South America had no problems whatsoever.[21]

In diction classes, some teachers—and a recent diction textbook— simply tell students to find preexisting translations and IPA, and use those. This is deficit teaching, the inability to carry out best practice in diction pedagogy. We have seen in Chapter 3 what happens if this kind of foundation is laid. When the time comes for singers to perform repertoire for which there is no preexisting translation or IPA, they have forgotten how to do the work on their own, and in the professional world are quickly left behind by those actively engaged with language.

Some colleagues argue that, if foreign languages are studied *after* diction classes, then students can apply the rules they learned, reinforcing them.[22] The problem, though, is that in these college language classes voice students are exposed to hours and hours of terrible pronunciation by classmates outside their field. While a native speaker may be leading the class, rarely is the teacher speaking consistently with formal pronunciation. Language teachers are always so pressed for time to cover a certain amount of material, that pronunciation receives the lowest priority, so there is little time for even a question about pronunciation.

A 21st-Century Approach for First-Year Students

Keeping in mind that some first-year English-speaking students have absolutely no background in studying a foreign language, and most have a superficial background with foreign languages, it is imperative that most first-year voice students study a college-level foreign language class their first year, along with a college-level English writing class. The study of Italian, German, or French at the college-level that first year will help orient students' brains toward L2 acquisition skills needed in diction classes; the English writing class, which involves extensive feedback and revisions, will make their spelling and attention to punctuation that much better. Ideally, first-year students are also studying in a basic IPA class with possibly English diction. Laying this kind of foundation will enable the diction teacher to focus on all best practice objectives during the sophomore year and later. Issues of grammar must still be confronted at the sophomore level, but sophomores are much more prepared academically, vocally, and in every other way. By moving out of compartmentalization and siloing that sophomore year—by setting up the possibility of adding some students from other class levels and related majors, and by moving into a virtual exchange—diction classes can be part of a transformational experience and help lay the foundation for students' long-term success.

The Italian Diction Dilemma

Nico Castel had a discussion with me once about his invitations to give guest masterclasses at various academic institutions. Often, he was asked to teach both French and German diction workshops during a single visit, but not Italian, or was scheduled half the amount of time for Italian as he was given for either French or German. He would plead with his hosts that he actually needed *twice* the amount of time for Italian![23]

68   *From Compartmentalization to Transformation*

Experienced diction teachers know that Italian is the most difficult to teach, and vocal coaches know that Italian always requires the most coaching time.[24] After students have taken the three diction courses, they usually have more problems reading an unknown Italian sentence than reading a line of text in German or even French. For English speakers, Italian inflection is by far the most difficult of the three, and the prevalence of Italian recitative makes for the biggest diction challenge of all. And yet, for native English speakers, Italian diction has the reputation for being the easiest of the three. This myth probably came about because Italian only has 7 vowel sounds, as opposed to the 15 of French or German. Also, because Italian is *the* basis for beautiful, classically trained singing, Italian songs are assigned early in a singer's development, usually in high school.

So, the argument is often that Italian diction should be studied first, and it should come as early as possible. For those of us teaching in the United States, can we examine this assumption for a moment? What if, along with English, Spanish songs were studied in a voice student's first semester instead? After all, Spanish is the second most widely spoken language in the USA, with 41 million people speaking Spanish at home;[25] most speakers of the language are underrepresented, so its study sends a strong message about "whose music matters"; there is a wealth of wonderful repertoire for all levels; it is the foreign language most studied by high school students, or by anyone in the country, by a huge margin; and with its five bright vowels, unaspirated consonants, and lack of long vowels, vowel clusters, and double consonants, it lays a great foundation before going on to Italian. Even Castel argued that Spanish is in several ways even more singable than Italian.[26] If not throughout the whole country, how about in at least the areas of the United States where there are large Hispanic populations, where non-Spanish speakers and Spanish speakers alike could share in this repertoire?[27]

If Spanish must wait until later, then when should Italian diction come into play? Steven Leigh, former professional opera singer and current Canadian Opera Company Ensemble Studio Lyric Diction Coach, has had the experience of designing and teaching a one-semester Italian diction class, as well as a separate full-year Italian language course for the Royal Conservatory of Music's Glenn Gould School. In his 2016 study, *Testing an Approach to Teaching Italian Lyric Diction to Opera Singers: An Action Research Study*, Leigh had an interesting proposal that was at the heart of his argument:

> My recommendation... is that once I have designed a one-year, four-language diction course, that it only be in the fourth year of

From Compartmentalization to Transformation 69

a singer's undergraduate studies. Only after having completed the three-language prerequisites, will the students be able to derive maximum benefit from the one-year diction course. Additionally, in their fourth year, singers should have a better understanding of their vocal mechanism, breath, and music styles... In other words, the diction class can do its job...[28]

Whether we agree or not that a diction class with four languages should wait until a student's last year of study, Leigh is definitely seeing the need for students to have the tools they require to focus on diction and to be able to retain their knowledge. But if waiting until the last year is one extreme, beginning the first year with a full-fledged Italian diction course is another extreme. One participant in Leigh's study was a 24-year-old singer who had taken Italian diction during her first year and said that this was not optimum because she felt she did not have control over what her voice was doing: "While it was useful at 18 to learn about IPA and how language worked, 10 minutes later, you didn't remember anything because your voice had changed."[29]

Add technical insecurity to lack of language study and hardly *any* grammar knowledge, plus a siloed class of first-year students, then it is no wonder that students do not retain much. I recently carried out a limited survey of ten singers who had graduated in the last ten years from a well-known conservatory that has a free curriculum (see Chapter 2). Students were free to take diction classes whenever they wanted, but they were required to take a first-semester IPA/English diction class. There was one other requirement—they had to complete one semester of the corresponding language before taking the diction class. I emailed the former students asking what choices they had made, and why, and whether they would have changed anything, and why. Students had based their choices on their advisor's recommendations, feedback from other students, and, of course, their own schedules (some were double majors). Advisors recommended that they take Italian diction the second semester of their first year, if at all possible. Fellow voice majors recommended they take French diction their senior year, "because it was the most complicated."[30] All of the respondents did take French diction their senior year, except for one, who took the class his junior year:

I think knowing basic grammar and how to identify the parts of speech in different languages because of the language classes helped a lot once I got to the diction course. I thought the timing of the diction classes themselves worked as well. If anything,

70 *From Compartmentalization to Transformation*

I would've liked to have completed them sooner, but, in hindsight, having French delayed until my Junior year, because of the language requirement, was helpful in deterring me from repertoire that was well beyond my capabilities that I would have probably tried to sing before I was ready if I was confident in my diction.[31]

Admittedly, this is a small sampling, but those who had taken Italian diction their second semester said that that was too soon, even after having had the introductory IPA/English class—either they were over-extended by experimenting with a second major, or they weren't secure enough vocally, or they just did not retain much of what they had learned. These students either did not test as being proficient in Italian diction when they began their graduate work, or they simply opted to take an Italian diction class again, from the ground up.[32]

Interestingly, the preferred order and timing from the sampling of students, with language study preceding the diction classes, came out as the following. (Remember that they were free to take the three foreign language classes whenever they wanted.) In some schools, this is what is set up as a fixed curriculum!:[33]

First year, first semester	Required IPA/English
Second year, second semester	Italian
Third year, second semester	German
Fourth year, second semester	French

Compartmentalization and Siloing: Why Did They Sell Their Books?!

Before the start of every semester, I would go to our campus bookstore to make sure the class diction textbooks had arrived. (This was when the bookstore actually stocked books.) I was always surprised to see how the books labeled "USED" significantly outnumbered the new books, year after year. Lyric diction is based on formal standards that apply to the pronunciation of texts covering hundreds of years, so it's not as if these books would be outdated anytime soon. I joked with my class that these used books must have been from singers who decided that a career in singing was just not for them. Seriously, I told my students not to sell their books, as they would need them throughout their whole careers.

This reminded me of a massage therapist who told me that one of her classmates in massage school had said "We're almost finished—I can't

From Compartmentalization to Transformation 71

wait to sell this textbook!" She replied, "Really? But that's when we'll need it the most, when we're practicing in the field!" Which person would you rather have as your massage therapist? All things equal, which singer would you rather listen to?

Yes, most students' books probably *should* be resold, and most college students are strapped for money.[34] Let's say, though, that it is financially possible to keep the books. In this case, lyric diction is so fundamental to a singer's career, that this huge inventory of used books shows us that a high percentage of students either *do* actually decide to forego a career in singing or teaching voice, or do not realize how important diction is to their career, or, perhaps, they assume that they now "know" diction, or at least know it well enough to rely on outside resources, including coaches, to provide the rest. Unfortunately, it is a lot of the latter.

When a first-year student enters into compartmentalized courses and is surrounded by other first-year students, it is almost impossible to gain perspective. The mindset is that if they get good grades in their individual classes, then they will come out a finished product in the end. As we have seen, the prevailing tendency for Generation Z students, too, is to turn to digital resources to find the quickest way to complete an assignment, and to skip steps that they perceive as being too time-consuming.[35] In a "myopic" class of only one class level, there are no older singers to serve as models and show them another way (see Chapter 3).

From kindergarten through elementary school, to middle and high school STEM and STEAM programs, to lower-level university undergraduate courses, and even up to the master's level, schools across the globe have been tackling the issues of compartmentalization and siloing, often following the lead of businesses and administrative units.[36]

The business model of breaking down silos can apply to music and voice departments, in which it is essential to create a unified vision, work toward a common goal, communicate, build trust, and create a thriving and productive team. Moreover, the business model methods for creating a thriving team can also apply within a diction class, which functions as a team. Key factors are knowledge, collaboration, creativity, and confidence,[37] addressed in Chapter 3.

In the voice curriculum, because of the development of different skill sets, compartmentalization is a particular pitfall. Integration of technique, diction, and acting skills is difficult under the best of circumstances. But how much of this difficulty is par for the course? I had originally prepared for this chapter many examples of how students' perspectives are primed for separating out their skills instead of

72 *From Compartmentalization to Transformation*

combining them, with the default being a focus on technique. But we all know this, or have experienced it ourselves, so I will be brief. As a diction coach, I know that I only need to enter the room in the midst of an opera scene run-through, and suddenly students' diction becomes much better, or the stage director can leave the room, and suddenly emphasis is more on music and following the conductor. One moment in diction class was very telling. When I had made clear my expectations for students to memorize their texts and translations, an undergraduate raised her hand and excitedly said, "Yes, I want to know my text so well that I don't have to think about it and I can concentrate on my technique!" It seemed to make so much sense to everyone that almost everyone nodded. But then I asked, "Wait a minute. Don't you want your technique to be so solid that you're free to focus on the text? Don't diction and technique go hand-in-hand to communicate the text?" There was a short moment of silence, and then an "Oh, of course!" moment from the class.

When our team of educators and teams of students keep in the forefront their common goal, then integration and wider perspectives can happen more easily. As seen in Chapter 2, Cashman's leading international lyric diction pedagogues clarified that goal beautifully, and it applies to both within and without a diction class: "They were unanimous in their conviction that communicating the meaning of a text while interpreting and expressing its emotional message is the goal of lyric diction and indeed of singing itself."[38]

Integration cannot just happen through a segmented progression of classes or outside workshops, no matter how good that may look on paper. Integration must happen from within classes, overlapping with one another, with the communication of text being the connecting thread throughout. We have already seen in Chapter 3 how a siloed review class for master's voice students who lack basic diction skills fails to take advantage of the perfect opportunity to add mixed-age diversity and a wide range of repertoire to an undergraduate diction class (that may also be completely siloed), which would then exponentially raise everyone's diction and critical listening skills, along with soft skills needed to thrive in today's world. In Chapter 4, we saw how a very intelligent and talented incoming doctoral student had fallen through the cracks with Italian diction and translating skills because of siloing, resulting in his overreliance on outside resources in order to stay afloat, which no one had apparently even realized.

Compartmentalization begins the first year, and if it continues past then, we are hampering students' potential. This is true whether it is voice, math, history, or any other field. For many schools, a student's

From Compartmentalization to Transformation 73

sophomore year is just as siloed as their first year, with the third and fourth years being devoted to exploring and attempting to integrate students' knowledge and skills. The second year, though, is the year to break free of compartmentalization as much as possible.

The Sophomore Year: An Opportunity for Exploration and Transformation

While much has been accomplished to provide first-year students with welcoming and supportive initiatives in their transition from high school to college, research into the university sophomore year has only come about in the last 20 years. It is a transitional year, with the potential to become a transformative one. Students emerge from their foundational first-year experience ready to explore and see where they might fit in, looking at their past, present, and their possible futures. As they assimilate into the larger academic community, they are ready and open to wider perspectives.[39]

In her 2005 pioneering article, Molly Schaller characterizes the sophomore year as "focused exploration," "a period of deep personal reflection about life and the future," a time "to develop a deep inner voice."[40] Whereas the first year is a time of non-focused, "random exploration," in which students explore the new world of college life, the second year should open up to focused exploration of the world around them, meaningful collaboration, and the possibilities for how they might envision themselves in the world. In Schaller's study, one sophomore, Dan, described the second-year experience particularly well:

'I think being a sophomore is more—you see both sides. I think it's almost like a turning point in a way.... It's like you're standing on a fence.' Dan's metaphor for standing on a fence fit what others in the study described: Sophomores look backward and see their first year of college and their childhood, and they look forward and see the rest of their college career and their future.[41]

It is a time for students to take more initiative, more responsibility for their learning. Schaller emphasizes that instructors should provide second-year students with opportunities to explore the world beyond the classroom and the school, possibly through study abroad or community work. She also advocates that they require these students to take time for self-reflection (a theme we have seen elsewhere in this book—see "Self-Recordings after the Pandemic" in Chapter 4; and

74 *From Compartmentalization to Transformation*

Chapter 6), in which they examine their own learning processes and take responsibility for their decisions.[42] Having laid a basic foundation of language study, English grammar, vocal technique, music theory, and music history during the first year, the sophomore year is the ideal—crucial—year, then, for voice majors to join with younger and older voice majors, conductors, and pianists, and break free of siloing. As was laid out in Chapter 1, a transformative, experiential diction class with a virtual exchange component opens up their perspective on a global scale and helps everyone to realize their common goals. This approach, too, according to research by Seemiller, Grace, and others, is exactly what today's students want—applied learning and skill-building that takes them beyond the classroom.[43]

Notes

1. Email to the author, May 15, 2021. Used with permission.
2. François Grosjean, "Can a Second Language Help You Learn a Third?," *Psychology Today*, June 2, 2015, https://www.psychologytoday.com/us/blog/life-bilingual/201506/can-second-language-help-you-learn-third.
3. Beverly Sills, foreword to Nico Castel, *French Opera Libretti in Two Volumes, Vol. I* (Mt. Morris, NY: Leyerle Publications, 1999): xiii.
4. I write here about Americans, but know that the skills of Canadians and Australians are similar.
5. Although, of course, most top universities require that entering students have studied at least two years of a foreign language in high school.
6. Kat Devlin, "Most European students are learning a foreign language in school while Americans lag," *Pew Research Center*, August 6, 2018, https://www.pewresearch.org/fact-tank/2018/08/06/most-european-students-are-learning-a-foreign-language-in-school-while-americans-lag/; and Kathleen Stein-Smith, "Foreign language classes becoming more scarce," *American Academy of Arts & Sciences*, February 6, 2019, https://www.amacad.org/news/foreign-language-classes-becoming-more-scarce.
7. "Foreign Language Requirements for College," *College Transitions*, updated August 2020, https://www.collegetransitions.com/dataverse/foreign-language-requirements.
8. See Gonzalez as one example of many: Jennifer Gonzalez, "How to Deal with Student Grammar Errors," *Cult of Pedagogy*, July 30, 2017, https://www.cultofpedagogy.com/grammar-spelling-errors/.
9. Ibid., and see Gonzalez's list of references.
10. Dana Goldstein, "Why Kids Can't Write," *New York Times*, August 2, 2017, https://www.nytimes.com/2017/08/02/education/edlife/writing-education-grammar-students-children.html.
11. Judit Pál and Camille Marec and Markus Schwabe, "United States-Country Note-PISA 2018 Results," *Programme for International Student Assessment (PISA)*. https://www.oecd.org/pisa/publications/PISA2018_CN_USA.pdf.

From Compartmentalization to Transformation 75

12. Dana Goldstein, "'It Just Isn't Working:' PISA Test Scores Cast Doubt on U.S. Education Efforts," *New York Times*, December 2, 2019, updated December 5, 2019, https://www.nytimes.com/2019/12/03/us/us-students-international-test-scores.html.
13. Although grammar in college foreign language classes usually comes into play during the second year of study, and undergraduate singers usually stop after one, maybe two semesters.
14. Again, many schools already have this kind of curriculum in place, but for different reasons. The crucial emphasis on language and grammar must be reinforced.
15. I now have grammar terminology sheets for all my diction classes, noting especially when grammar can effect pronunciation. I keep the terminology very basic, enough that is essential for a singer's profession, using comparisons to English grammar.
16. Goldstein, "Why Kids Can't Write."
17. For example, on pp. 32–33, "Carefully copy the following text, including all accent marks and underlines ..." Thomas Grubb, *Singing in French* (New York: G. Schirmer, 1979), 32–33.
18. Corey Seemiller and Meghan Grace, *Generation Z: A Century in the Making* (New York: Routledge, 2019), 236.
19. John Anderer, "The Pen is Mightier than the Keyboard: Writing by Hand Helps us Learn, Remember More," *StudyFinds*, October 5, 2020, https://www.studyfinds.org/writing-by-hand-better-for-brain/.
20. This pertained to second-semester language classes in French, Italian, and German studied in the junior and senior years!
21. Email to the author on June 3, 2021. Used by permission.
22. One is Cheri Montgomery, in "Diction (Still) Belongs in the Music Department," *Journal of Singing: The Official Journal of the National Association of Teachers of Singing* 76, no. 3 (January/February 2020): 308. However, she does acknowledge the need to know something about Italian grammar in order to be able to look up the conjugations of verbs to find the pronunciation of stressed *e*'s and *o*'s: See Cheri Montgomery, *Italian Lyric Diction Workbook: Teacher's Manual* (Nashville, TN: S.T.M. Publishers, 2009), 24, 134.
23. Conversation with the author at Albion College, Michigan, fall of 1996.
24. One need only ask vocal coaches! Coach Marcie Stapp, for example, wrote that Italian repertoire, specifically its diction, "... consistently requires the most coaching time." Marcie Stapp, *The Singer's Guide to Languages* (San Francisco, CA: Teddy's Music Press, 1996) 87.
25. "Spanish Language in the United States," *Wikipedia*, accessed June 7, 2021, https://en.wikipedia.org/wiki/Spanish_language_in_the_United_States.
26. Nico Castel, *A Singer's Manual of Spanish Lyric Diction* (New York: Excalibur Books, 1994), 3–4.
27. Spanish speakers could also learn songs from different regions, with different pronunciations than they are used to.
28. Steven Alan Leigh, "Testing an Approach to Teaching Italian Lyric Diction to Opera Singers: An Action Research Study" (MA thesis, University of Toronto, 2016), 115. Available at https://tspace.library.utoronto.ca/bitstream/1807/72743/1/Leigh_Steven_A_201606_MA_thesis.pdf.
29. Ibid., p. 106.

76 *From Compartmentalization to Transformation*

30. Email to the author, May 12, 2021. Used with permission.
31. Email to the author, May 17, 2021. Used with permission.
32. Two exceptions were a student who had attended a high school for the arts and had extensive Italian diction and IPA there, and a student who was a double major in computer science and voice who took no diction classes at all his first year, not even the required introductory one.
33. I certainly understand the reasoning to place Italian first among foreign languages, but I would recommend strongly considering that German diction be first, after English. Because the languages are related, German proceeds naturally from English (and see Amanda Johnston's approach to combining the two in her *English and German Diction for Singers: A Comparative Approach.* 2nd ed. (Lanham, MD: Rowman & Littlefield, 2016); German is extremely phonetic, with very clear-cut rules and relatively few exceptions; students learn a lot more IPA than they would in Italian, and much of it will also apply to French; they must still sing with a bright, forward placement; German inflection is similar to English; expression in German is similar to English, using expressive consonants; and they become aware of vowel length, setting them up for Italian, where vowel length is crucial. Italian diction would be next, when they have a good foundational vocal technique and a good legato, and are ready to dive into all the intricacies of Italian diction.
34. Paul T. Corrigan, "Students, Keep Your Books" *Inside Higher Ed*, June 3, 2016, https://www.insidehighered.com/views/2016/06/03/enduring-power-textbooks-students-lives-essay.
35. Seemiller and Grace, *Generation Z*, 203, 236.
36. For the business world, see: Brent Gleeson, "The Silo Mentality: How to Break Down the Barriers," *Forbes*, October 2, 2013, https://www.forbes.com/sites/brentgleeson/2013/10/02/the-silo-mentality-how-to-break-down-the-barriers/?sh=32bb371e8c7e.
    For an excellent look at solutions to K–12 siloing see: Alexandra Owens, "Tearing Down the Silos in K–12 Curricula," *ASCD in Service*, January 24, 2017, https://inservice.ascd.org/tearing-down-the-silos-in-k-12-curricula/.
    For a look at reorganizing siloed college administrative units to benefit students, see: Ryan Craig, "College Silos Must Die for Students to Thrive," *Forbes*, April 14, 2017, https://www.forbes.com/sites/ryan-craig/2017/04/14/college-silos-must-die-for-students-to-thrive/?sh=c-c50e01222dd.
    For an interdisciplinary approach to a first-year entry-level sustainability course, see: Nicholas Coops and Jean Marcus and Ileana Construt and Erica Frank and Ron Kellet and Eric Mazzi and Susan Nesbit and Andrew Riseman and John Robinson and Anneliese Schultz and Yona Sipos, "How an entry-level, interdisciplinary sustainability course revealed the benefits and challenges of a university-wide initiative for sustainability education," *International Journal of Sustainability in Higher Education* 16, no. 5 (2015): 729–747.
37. Gleeson, "The Silo Mentality."
38. Penelope Cashman, "International Best Practice in the Teaching of Lyric Diction to Conservatorium-Level Singers" (PhD diss., Elder Conservatorium of Music, University of Adelaide, 2019), 289. Available at https://digital.library.adelaide.edu.au/dspace/handle/2440/120990.

From Compartmentalization to Transformation 77

39. See Laurie A. Schreiner and Sharyn Slavin Miller and Tamera L. Pullins and Troy L. Seppelt, "Beyond Sophomore Survival," in *Thriving in Transitions: A Research-Based Approach to College Student Success,* ed. L.A. Schreiner, M.C. Louis, and D.D. Nelson (Columbia, SC: University of South Carolina, National Resource Center for the First-Year Experience and Students in Transition, 2012), 111–136.
40. Molly A. Schaller, "Wandering and Wondering: Traversing the Uneven Terrain of the Second College Year," *About Campus* (July–August, 2005): 18–19, 22. Available at http://www.secondyear.umn.edu/files/Schaller%20-%202005%20-%20Wandering%20and%20wondering%20Traversing%20the%20uneven%20ter.pdf.
41. Ibid., p. 19.
42. Ibid., p. 23.
43. Students are not impressed by marketing catchphrases such as "premier institution" or "tight-knit community," but prefer above all schools that advertise "hands-on learning" and "real-world experience." Seemiller and Grace, *Generation Z*, 204.

Bibliography

Anderer, John. *"The Pen is Mightier Than the Keyboard: Writing by Hand Helps us Learn, Remember More."* *StudyFinds*, October 5, 2020. https://www.studyfinds.org/writing-by-hand-better-for-brain/.

Cashman, Penelope. *"International Best Practice in the Teaching of Lyric Diction to Conservatorium-Level Singers."* PhD diss., Elder Conservatorium of Music, University of Adelaide, 2019. Available at https://digital.library.adelaide.edu.au/dspace/handle/2440/120990.

Castel, Nico. *A Singer's Manual of Spanish Lyric Diction*. New York: Excalibur Books, 1994.

Coops, Nicholas, Jean Marcus, Ileana Construt, Erica Frank, Ron Kellet, Eric Mazzi, Susan Nesbit, Andrew Riseman, John Robinson, Anneliese Schultz, and Yona Sipos. "How an Entry-Level, Interdisciplinary Sustainability Course Revealed the Benefits and Challenges of a University-Wide Initiative for Sustainability Education." *International Journal of Sustainability in Higher Education* 16, no. 5 (2015): 729–747.

Corrigan, Paul T. "Students, Keep Your Books." *Inside Higher Ed*, June 3, 2016. https://www.insidehighered.com/views/2016/06/03/enduring-power-textbooks-students-lives-essay.

Craig, Ryan. "College Silos Must Die for Students to Thrive." *Forbes*, April 14, 2017. https://www.forbes.com/sites/ryancraig/2017/04/14/college-silos-must-die-for-students-to-thrive/?sh=cc50e01222dd.

Devlin, Kat. "Most European students are learning a foreign language in school while Americans lag." *Pew Research Center*. August 6, 2018. https://www.pewresearch.org/fact-tank/2018/08/06/most-european-students-are-learning-a-foreign-language-in-school-while-americans-lag.

"Foreign Language Requirements for College." *College Transitions*. Updated August 2020. https://www.collegetransitions.com/dataverse/foreign-language-requirements.

78 *From Compartmentalization to Transformation*

Gleeson, Brent. "The Silo Mentality: How to Break Down the Barriers." *Forbes*, October 2, 2013. https://www.forbes.com/sites/brentgleeson/2013/10/02/the-silo-mentality-how-to-break-down-the-barriers/?sh=32bb371e8c7e.

Goldstein, Dana. "'It Just Isn't Working:' PISA Test Scores Cast Doubt on U.S. Education Efforts." *New York Times*, December 2, 2019, updated December 5, 2019. https://www.nytimes.com/2019/12/03/us/us-students-international-test-scores.html.

_____. "Why Kids Can't Write." *New York Times*, August 2, 2017. https://www.nytimes.com/2017/08/02/education/edlife/writing-education-grammar-students-children.html.

Gonzalez, Jennifer. "How to Deal with Student Grammar Errors." *Cult of Pedagogy*, July 30, 2017. https://www.cultofpedagogy.com/grammar-spelling-errors/.

Grosjean, François. "Can a Second Language Help You Learn a Third?" *Psychology Today*, June 2, 2015. https://www.psychologytoday.com/us/blog/life-bilingual/201506/can-second-language-help-you-learn-third Accessed on June 2, 2021.

Grubb, Thomas. *Singing in French*. New York: G. Schirmer, 1979.

Johnston, Amanda. *English and German Diction for Singers: A Comparative Approach*. 2nd ed. Lanham, MD: Rowman & Littlefield, 2016.

Leigh, Steven Alan. "Testing an Approach to Teaching Italian Lyric Diction to Opera Singers: An Action Research Study." MA thesis, University of Toronto, 2016. Available at https://tspace.library.utoronto.ca/bitstream/1807/72743/1/Leigh_Steven_A_201606_MA_thesis.pdf.

Montgomery, Cheri. "Diction (Still) Belongs in the Music Department." *Journal of Singing: The Official Journal of the National Association of Teachers of Singing* 76, no. 3 (January/February 2020): 301–309.

_____. *Italian Lyric Diction Workbook: Teacher's Manual*. Nashville, TN: S.T.M. Publishers, 2009.

Owens, Alexandra. "Tearing Down the Silos in K-12 Curricula." *ASCD in Service*, January 24, 2017. https://inservice.ascd.org/tearing-down-the-silos-in-k-12-curricula/.

Pál, Judit, Camille Marec, and Markus Schwabe. "United States-Country Note-PISA 2018 Results." *Programme for International Student Assessment (PISA)*. 2019. https://www.oecd.org/pisa/publications/PISA2018_CN_USA.pdf.

Schaller, Molly A. "Wandering and Wondering: Traversing the Uneven Terrain of the Second College Year." *About Campus* (July–August, 2005): 17–24. Available at http://www.secondyear.umn.edu/files/Schaller%20-%202005%20-%20Wandering%20and%20wondering%20Traversing%20the%20uneven%20ter.pdf.

Schreiner, Laurie A., Sharyn Slavin Miller, Tamera L. Pullins, and Troy L. Seppelt "Beyond Sophomore Survival." In *Thriving in Transitions: A Research-Based Approach to College Student Success*, edited by L.A. Schreiner, M.C. Louis,

From Compartmentalization to Transformation 79

and D.D. Nelson, 111–136. Columbia, SC: University of South Carolina, National Resource Center for the First-Year Experience and Students in Transition, 2012.

Seemiller, Corey, and Meghan Grace. *Generation Z: A Century in the Making.* New York: Routledge, 2019.

Sills, Beverly. Foreword to Castel, Nico. *French Opera Libretti in Two Volumes, Vol. I.* Mt. Morris, NY: Leyerle Publications, 1999.

Stapp, Marcie. *The Singer's Guide to Languages.* San Francisco, CA: Teddy's Music Press, 1996.

Stein-Smith, Kathleen. "Foreign language classes becoming more scarce." *American Academy of Arts & Sciences*, February 6, 2019. https://www.amacad.org/news/foreign-language-classes-becoming-more-scarce.

Wikipedia. "Spanish Language in the United States." Accessed June 7, 2021. https://en.wikipedia.org/wiki/Spanish_language_in_the_United_States.

6 Virtual Exchange
A Window to the 21st Century

> You've got a pool of talented young people attempting to master an art form that is increasingly foreign to them in terms of the language and musical style.
>
> (George Shirley, world-renowned tenor)[1]

> *How can we be as diverse, equitable, and inclusive as possible?*
> *How can we best make use of technology in our hybrid world?*
> *Whose music matters?*
> *How can we best nurture curiosity and collaboration, preferably on a global scale?*
> *How can we best foster independence?*
> *How can we avoid compartmentalization and siloing?*
> *How can DEI and 21st-century elements be assimilated within a class?*

Now we have come full circle and see that what appear to be narrow, specialized, Eurocentric courses on the surface can be opened up, taken out of a compartmentalized environment, moved to their most diverse level, and utilized for their full potential. Diction classes are definitely skill-oriented, but we see clearly that the skills that are able to be developed are as much soft skills as hard ones. The next natural step is a virtual exchange, which skyrockets classes to new levels. These kinds of diction classes, then, are truly for the 21st century, and they come about from substantive changes from *within* the courses themselves. They answer *all* of the above questions, and more, as was put forth in Chapter 1.

How to spark students' curiosity and help them to develop a lifelong fascination and love for other languages and cultures?

These are the most successful singers, the most successful and fulfilled artists! In Chapter 2, it was seen from Penelope Cashman's recent study that this pedagogical goal is one of best practice by diction

DOI: 10.4324/9781003226208-7

Virtual Exchange 81

teachers worldwide.[2] If that fire is not lit, students usually develop a habit of simply relying on outside resources that provide IPA and translations, instead of attempting any of the work themselves *before* utilizing these great supplementary tools. As a result, they rise to a certain level, but never progress further in the professional world.

How can students better bridge the gap among learning Italian, German, and French pronunciation while isolated in an American classroom, and direct communication in these languages in front of an audience? Can that moment of genuine, direct communication happen in the classroom?

Yes, through the experiential learning environment of virtual exchange! And this learning environment, as we saw in Chapter 5, must be set up so that it is as diverse as possible, occurring after a foundation of foreign language study, English writing skills, and a basic vocal technique have been laid during the first year.

How to place a specialized, Eurocentric university course in context for the student, beyond the school's walls? And, can we shift the centrism to allow for even more layers of growth?

Through technology, this can be done. Sounds and translations can be brought almost immediately into context by connecting with foreign peers and communicating texts to them directly. Centrism can be shifted through an equal exchange, in this case through an exchange with songs by African American composers, further bringing students' work into perspective.

How to better engage students, further develop skills, and more confidently assure student retention of knowledge?

Students tend to enter college into a compartmentalized environment, no matter how integrated our courses look on paper. They enter college ready to check off boxes and be finished with classes. A wider perspective and genuine integration are crucial. Again, as we saw in Chapter 5, an introductory diction class is ideal for first-year students, along with their first college-level foreign language and English writing classes, not to mention the formative, technical work they carry out with their private voice teachers. This leads directly to transformative, exploratory, experiential, diverse diction classes that carry virtual exchanges, from the sophomore level on up.

How to widen perspectives, develop initiative, independence, and social and intercultural skills?

None of these goals needs to be shifted to outside workshops, as valuable as they are, or other classes. They can happen *within* a diction class. If they can happen within a class, why compartmentalize and silo the class, when both the hard skills of diction and the soft skills of social interaction can complement and advance one another?

82 *Virtual Exchange*

How to help lay a groundwork for a student's international collaboration?

This no longer has to wait for participation in European summer programs, which not everyone has the opportunity to benefit from. Collaboration through a virtual exchange happens with European peers who speak the language, instead of with a group of peers in a summer program who do not. For those fortunate enough to have a semester abroad, the groundwork can now be laid beforehand within their home institution.

Many readers have probably already had the experience of hosting or teaching in an international virtual masterclass. For a diction class, this is of enormous value, as students learn from a native speaker who is also an experienced singer, voice teacher, or vocal coach. The experience also helps put the class in context, giving students the perspective that the language they are learning to communicate in is not restricted to English-speaking peers in their classroom or school, or English-speaking audiences in their city, state, or country. Of course, they knew this intellectually, but their day-to-day routine and lack of international experience misled them to think otherwise.

Study abroad, either a whole semester or in a summer program, can be a life-changing experience for students. The vast majority of students, however, do not have the opportunity to spend a semester abroad. For those able to participate in international summer programs, they are exposed to entirely different cultures and intense, immersive learning experiences. In terms of raising students' consciousness about music and culture, more can be accomplished in a four-week program overseas than in four years in a university at home. While these programs enhance and build upon what students learn in their schools, they are still separate experiences from their more regimented academic ones, so that upon return to their home country, they are unable to sustain the level of absorption they experienced abroad. Also, immersion in a summer program usually means immersion alongside other English speakers, or with some participating students from other countries except students from the country they are studying in.

Diction classes with virtual exchanges, in which students collaborate independently with foreign peers in equal exchanges, are a real game-changer, opening up enormous possibilities for growth. Unlike study abroad, available to the fortunate few, virtual exchanges can equitably benefit everyone in the classroom. The possibilities are far-reaching, and the classes can add the international virtual masterclass element, motivate some students to pursue study abroad, and help prepare all the students not only with the hard skills of diction and language, but also with the soft skills of international collaboration.

Chapter 1 laid out a transformative Italian diction class that had already been functioning at its most diverse and collaborative level. This chapter looks at the details of setting up and engaging in a virtual exchange post-pandemic, addresses misgivings, and lays out the hard, soft, and digital skills developed in such a diction class. This chapter also advocates for the study of songs by African American and other underrepresented composers as a major component of virtual exchanges.

Virtual Exchange: What It Is Not, and What It Is

Toward the beginning of the pandemic, many academic organizations in the United States turned to NAFSA: Association of International Educators, whose primary goal is to advance international education and exchange.[3] Numerous educators were seeking ways to initiate virtual exchanges as an attempt to quickly incorporate international experiences into their newly online courses. Experts at NAFSA, however, pointed out that setting up virtual exchanges was not a simple, quick process.

First, let's look at what virtual exchanges are *not*. Virtual exchanges are not distance-learning courses. They also have nothing to do with social media. They are not programs that lack a sustained pedagogy for interaction, such as a course that incorporates one or two masterclasses. On the contrary, Philomena Meechan and Todd L. Austin, heads of the University of Michigan Virtual Exchange Initiative, made it clear to me that there must be at least five full joint-class meetings in order to successfully integrate an effective, meaningful exchange into a course. Crucial components of virtual exchanges include the following:

- Truly equal exchanges. Student partners on both sides must equally benefit from the experience, although the *way* they benefit can be different. This means that both faculty partners must be equally involved in planning.
- Faculty need to be trained, to be led through the process, in order to make sure the exchange is well planned, and to be able to facilitate collaboration among students. At the University of Michigan, this involved about ten hours of online training during the summer by our Virtual Exchange Initiative, with input from other faculty who have been utilizing virtual exchanges for several years or

84   *Virtual Exchange*

more. This training involved myself, my international partner, and other teams in various disciplines who were initiating exchanges. Our Initiative also researched several technologies for us to try and followed up with us throughout our course to offer guidance and suggestions.

- The virtual exchange must involve an initial "meet-and-greet," an opportunity to break the ice and for students to get to know one another.
- The exchange must make clear to students what is expected of them. Students' one-on-one work must be purposeful, intentional, with expected, reflective feedback and self-evaluation. Some ideas are presented in this chapter.
- In addition to the students working independently, outside of class, the combined classes must meet virtually at least five times to observe and discuss what is being learned. For diction classes, this is where a basic masterclass format can come into play.
- There must be a final debriefing with the combined classes, with input and feedback from students, so that they gain an overall perspective of what their collaboration has achieved. Written responses are also helpful to faculty and help to make sure that students take the time to reflect.
- Faculty partners must meet to evaluate the course and discuss ways to build upon their exchange.[4]

Across the Ocean: Erasmus+ and Virtual Exchange

In 1987, the Erasmus Program was launched as a student exchange program among member countries of the European Union. It was highly successful and expanded to become Erasmus+, serving not only educational and cultural exchanges between international university students, but also lifelong learning for older adults, youth programs, and internships with businesses. It has even expanded to include some institutions outside the 27 countries of the European Union. The Erasmus+ 2021–2027 project goes even further, with a focus on social inclusion, digital skills, artificial intelligence, clean energy, and climate change. There is a strong emphasis on including more people with disabilities, people of different ages, and those from diverse cultural, social, and economic backgrounds. Some of the objectives of Erasmus+ sound very familiar to our ears: "… it enhances knowledge, skills, and attitudes, improves employability, helps confidence-building and independence, stimulates curiosity and innovation, fosters the understanding of other people…"[5] Almost 5,000 institutions across

Virtual Exchange 85

the EU participate in Erasmus+, and courses taken outside of one's home country are easily counted toward the home school's degree. The average length of study for an Erasmus+ student is six months, with the majority being undergraduates, although almost one third are master's students.[6] Professor Leonardo De Lisi, Vice Director of the Conservatorio Luigi Cherubini in Florence, and my virtual exchange partner, stated that about 60–65% of his Italian voice students participate in the Erasmus+ program, studying a semester abroad, usually in France, Germany, Austria, or England.[7]

College students in the United States who studied abroad for credit in 2018–2019, before the pandemic, numbered 347,099.[8] This is an increase of 1.6% over the previous year, but even if we subtract the total number of international students in the United States' universities,[9] this represents only 1.85% of American college students, and most of these 1.85% are in STEM fields, followed by Business and Management, followed by Social Studies.[10]

All of this means several things for our diction classes and virtual exchanges. First, it drives home the huge difference between Europeans' and North Americans' opportunities for cultural and educational exchange, as well as the huge difference in language learning, as addressed in Chapter 5. Not only do English-speaking singers enter college with little to no foreign language skills, but they also tend to attain a bare minimum of study, if that, while in college. Many of America's study abroad programs, too, are in overseas branches of home institutions, so that even when students study abroad, almost all their classes are in English, and they are surrounded by other English speakers. For the sake of an English-speaking voice student's development and employability, much more emphasis should be placed on foreign language instruction in North America. Yes, it is very difficult to squeeze in more language study into a college academic year, but young American singers almost never seem to even consider summer intensive language study as an option, rather than study in, perhaps, a less-regarded summer opera program that is more about getting a show up on its feet at all costs than about creating a great learning experience that centers on process. In this case, what would be much more impressive on students' resumes would be the fact that they had studied intensive Italian for a month at the Università per stranieri in Perugia,[11] or any summer language immersion program at the Middlebury Language School in Vermont, in which participants must sign Middlebury's famous pledge not to speak any English during their entire stay, inside or outside the classroom. Middlebury's German for Singers summer

86 *Virtual Exchange*

program, too, combines four hours a day of language and diction study with coachings, opera scenes work, lectures, and other activities, on top of Middlebury's pledge.[12] There is also the Goethe Institute, and plenty of other language summer programs. If students are planning to participate in a summer European vocal program, they should be encouraged to pursue intense language study in Europe before or after the program, going beyond whatever language classes the vocal program might offer.

Language is great for singers to study while they are waiting for their voices to mature and are still building technique. Virtual exchanges have the distinct possibility of inspiring and motivating English-speaking students to pursue intense language study and even study abroad. This is, in fact, exactly what happened in my diction classes that incorporated virtual exchanges, discussed in this chapter (see "Longer-Term Outcomes").

The Erasmus+ program also means that Europeans are more in tune than ever before with international collaboration. Professor De Lisi's art song/diction class in Florence was made up of students from not only Erasmus+ countries in the European Union, but also from Turkey, New Zealand, Mexico, China, and the United States. Similarly, my virtual exchange partner in Germany at the Hochschule für Musik Nürnberg adds a regular stream of Erasmus+ foreign voice students to her studio of German singers, as well as singers from Korea and Russia. Does this mean, then, that the prospect of having virtual exchanges with students in North America offers nothing new to Europeans? Far from it. It means that Europeans are experienced with multicultural interaction and collaboration and are not only comfortable with it but also understand and appreciate its benefits. European students are quite eager, open, and curious to meet and work with fellow students from the United States, Canada, and elsewhere, and to learn new repertoire with the help of like-minded, native speaking peers.

Many European institutions are also now well-versed in cross-border virtual exchanges, especially since the pandemic. The groundwork for virtual exchange in the EU had been laid well beforehand, with multi-national support and dissemination of information about virtual exchange culminating right around the time of the pandemic. In 2014–2015, the European Commission (the executive branch of the European Union) had seen a "shift toward a more student-centered approach in teaching and learning within higher education" and sought ways of supporting technology-enhanced education. Some advantages cited were "blending classroom and virtual higher education,"

Virtual Exchange 87

"cross-border cooperation between institutions," and the "mainstreaming of a more interactive teaching and learning experience." The commission carried out a study "to provide research analysis for, and recommendations to, European governments that would aid them in promoting greater innovation in pedagogy and in the use of technology in higher education."[13] Part of the results of the Commission's recommendations led to project EVOLVE (Evidence-Validated Online Learning through Virtual Exchange), meant "to mainstream Virtual Exchange as an innovative form of collaborative international learning across disciplines in Higher Education institutions in Europe and beyond." EVOLVE was set up in 2018, was linked with Erasmus+, and officially ended its dissemination project on May 12, 2021.[14] Like NAFSA in the United States, EVOLVE's services in Europe were in high demand during the pandemic. EVOLVE described well a virtual exchange from the European perspective:

- It is sustained, unfolding over time with regular, intensive interaction.
- It involves regular synchronous meetings.
- It involves inclusive, intercultural collaboration and dialogue that inspires action with a long-term positive impact on relationships.
- It is learner-led, following the philosophy of dialogue where participants are the main recipients and the main drivers of knowledge; learning through dialogue means that participants will be seeking mutual understanding and co-creating knowledge, based on their own experiences.
- It is supported by trained facilitators and educators.
- It is integrated into formal educational programs.
- It is structured to foster mutual understanding, covering topics related to identity, empathy, perspective taking, critical reflection, and intercultural understanding.

For this final point, EVOLVE noted that a key tenet of virtual exchange is that "intercultural understanding and awareness are not automatic outcomes of contact between different groups/cultures."[15] This is a very important point, to be taken up later—faculty must prepare participants beforehand, to help them benefit the most from their collaboration; check on them periodically to see how the exchange is unfolding; and make sure they engage in critical reflection at the end of the course. In addition, feedback about what was learned in the collaboration, in front of the whole class, is beneficial for everyone.

88   *Virtual Exchange*

Addressing Misgivings

> *There is never enough time in a diction class* (see Chapter 2)*! How could I possibly add a virtual exchange component that takes up a whole class for meet-and-greet, another for debriefing, and time to hear Europeans singing in English?!*

This was certainly one of my misgivings, and it turns out that finding time in the syllabus for a virtual exchange is a fear of quite a few teachers across disciplines. If you are in the process of pleading for more hours per week for your diction classes, this can add to your argument. In any case, unless you are constrained to teach diction for three languages in one semester, time *can* be found. Carefully planned asynchronous lectures can free up class time. Cutting corners elsewhere are well worth the effort. Try redoing your syllabus with the goal of building toward the virtual exchange during the second half of the semester, so that the exchange is built into the course itself and not added on.

> *What about the logistics—the difference in time zones, the difference in semesters and holidays, students' complicated schedules on both sides of the ocean, equipment and connections that might not work, and cultural differences?!*

We have all learned during the pandemic that nothing is perfect, but what can be accomplished online is pretty amazing. As NAFSA notes, while logistics can be tricky, "that is a feature, not a bug."[16] The very act of navigating these challenges is a great learning experience for students. It helps their digital competence, their time management skills, their sensitivity to cultural differences, their communication skills, widens their perspective, helps them to become more independent, and helps them to take more initiative.

Logistically, the different time zones are not bad. At six hours apart, a North American diction class in the morning or afternoon can line up with an afternoon or evening meeting time in Europe.[17] (Those in South Africa are in the same time zone as Europe.) The semesters actually line up well, too, at least between North America and Europe. In Italy, Germany, and Austria, the school year for music schools begins November 1. (In France, it varies between mid-September and mid-October.) In North America, for a single-language semester-long diction class, this means that we can teach the first half of the fall semester as usual, with our students learning sounds, IPA, and rules. The initial virtual exchange meeting (the "meet-and-greet") can occur

Virtual Exchange 89

first thing in November. Select North American students can then meet independently with their foreign partners and be ready to sing in the second half of November. The foreign students will be ready to sing toward the very end of the North American semester. The winter semester is a little trickier because European schools don't usually begin their semester until March 1, and North American spring breaks and European Easter breaks often don't line up. It is still certainly doable, however, and it leaves plenty of time for the first half of the diction class to lay a solid groundwork of sounds, IPA, and rules before venturing into the virtual exchange element. In my latest exchange with Germany, the faculty member and students were so gracious and eager that they met us on Zoom in February, from their individual homes during their break, for the initial meet-and-greet![18]

As for students' class and work schedules, yes, this can be problematic, especially given the time difference. Although both my and Professor De Lisi's students noted this issue, students were all still able to find times to meet. All said, it was more than worth the effort and in the end was not a big issue. Students usually made use of both synchronous and asynchronous meetings. First, they found an initial time to connect live. Then, they sent recordings back and forth for feedback. Then, they met again live. This gave them more flexibility with their schedules and was a great use of technology!

As for equipment and connections, Europeans and their institutions basically had the same pandemic experiences with technology as everyone else. We are all equally technology-savvy, we have the same range of resources, and we are equally understanding and flexible about technological limitations and mishaps. Whatever technological advances lay ahead, we will all continue to learn from one another on both sides of the ocean as we experiment with them.

Finally, as for cultural differences, this is, of course, a huge plus.

Are my students mature enough to work independently with foreign students, and to follow through with making contact and carrying out independent work?

My approach was to begin with the oldest voice majors and work down. The older ones are the closest to giving degree recitals, as well, so this kind of work helps the immediate preparation for their recitals. So far, I have only involved five singers at a time. My goal is for all students to have the experience of collaborating one-on-one through a virtual exchange at some point in one of their three foreign language diction classes. Since I teach all three classes, I get to know all the

90 *Virtual Exchange*

students, their maturity levels, and needs. In the future, I may try to have a mix of, say, sophomores, juniors, and master's students. As a whole, I would say that first-year American students are not ready to work so autonomously with foreign peers, because of their maturity level and the burdens and newness of their first year, but there are certainly exceptions. In any case, it is important for the teachers (the "facilitators") on both sides to communicate with all students and give them guidance throughout their independent exchanges.

What if my faculty partner ventures into vocal technique?!

This is why there is planning, and why a good working relationship and understanding is built between partners before the class occurs. Partners make clear to one another that talking about vocal technique is off-limits. Students on both sides know, too, that their focus is on pronunciation and inflection, limited technically to talking about articulators, besides explaining the meaning of texts, style, and culture, and then onto whatever conversation naturally unfolds.

Finally, as with any class, life happens—students get sick, become overwhelmed, or crises occur. If or when any of these happen, we all understand and empathize. The depth of learning and growth that occurs in these collaborative exchanges easily absorbs any problems that may occur along the way and can add to our growth and understanding.

Won't there be a language barrier?

Faculty partners must have a mutual language in which they can communicate, of course. Students must be paired with students they can communicate with, but this is rarely a problem, given Europeans' overall ability to speak English. European students will probably appreciate the opportunity to practice their English, as well. It is certainly possible, though, that a native English speaker will know the European language well enough to converse in it. In any regard, students *will* learn about one another's languages at various levels, which is one of the benefits of the exchange.

But native speakers often don't know how they produce their sounds, often don't know IPA, and might not know formal rules for their own language!

For Italian, even with Italy's history of inconsistent lyric pronunciation due to so many dialects, Italian conservatories today, across the

Virtual Exchange 91

country, are very methodical in teaching the rules of formal Standard Italian pronunciation. All the Italian singers in our exchange had exemplary diction, knew the rules—including phrasal doublings—and were super-helpful with my students. They could not only demonstrate but also gave written feedback online and, being trained singers, could explain well enough if a sound was not quite right. The same was true of German student singers with Hochdeutsch. Italian and German voice teachers then further refine and explain details in the joint Zoom masterclass. (A French exchange is yet to be explored.) IPA at this stage, in this kind of exchange, isn't necessary.

Laying the Groundwork: Faculty Partners

Faculty partnerships are critical to the success of a virtual exchange, and partnerships take time to develop, especially long-distance over Zoom. I was fortunate to have already known and collaborated with my virtual exchange faculty partner, Leonardo De Lisi, for over 30 years. In fact, quite a few virtual exchanges involve existing relationships.[19] This, of course, meant that we did not need to take the time to get to know one another and could immediately dive into planning, bounce off ideas, and immerse ourselves in my school's training sessions. After the success of our Italian/American virtual exchange, Leonardo introduced me to a German colleague he had worked with for some time, helping me set up a virtual exchange for my German diction class (while he set up a German/Italian virtual exchange). Since my new German colleague and I were working together for the first time, we agreed that our first step would simply be an exchange of virtual masterclasses involving five of my students singing German songs and arias, and five of her students singing American songs and arias. We did begin with a meet-and-greet session, however, and met four more times throughout the winter semester for the masterclasses. We also had a debriefing session during our last meeting.

This initial step allowed my partner and me to get to know one another, while still very much helping to bring our classes into perspective for the students. One impromptu email from one of my students corroborated this: "... it means something different when you sing text to someone who understands it. It was amazing to see in her eyes, and her students, understanding."[20] The telling moment came during the debriefing session. Students were very enthusiastic about what they had learned, and especially about having had the opportunity to learn from knowledgeable native speakers. Then, my partner and I suggested that we would like to take the next step the following year and have a true virtual exchange,

92 *Virtual Exchange*

with students first learning from one another, independently, before performing for the combined classes. We asked what they thought of this, and they immediately responded with an excited "Yes!"

The virtual exchange with the conservatory in Florence involved my one-semester Italian diction class of 20 students, and Professor De Lisi's full-year art song/diction class of 18 students, ages 19–40. The exchange with the Musikhochschule in Germany involved my one-semester German diction class and a voice studio in Nürnberg of 20 students, ages 19–25. For those of you who have no preexisting ties or referrals, plenty of research into possible faculty collaborators can be carried out online. Also, the virtual exchange offices at home institutions are ready to help with finding partners. In Italy, there are 66 music schools of higher education, of which 55 are conservatories and 11 are music schools of equal stature.[21] In Germany, there are 24 Musikhochschulen[22]; and there are conservatories and music academies throughout Austria—in Graz, Linz, Salzburg, Vienna, Tirol, Eisenstadt, and Klagenfurt.[23] There are over 25 music schools of higher education in France.[24] Given the number of voice teachers and their studios, as well as vocal literature classes, then, finding a suitable faculty partner should be very possible.

Facilitator Training

For those academic institutions that have not yet established a virtual exchange department, SUNY COIL is a well-established leader in bringing virtual exchange to campuses worldwide. COIL offers training and help for individual teachers, as well as consultations and services for campus administrators. For teachers, they give this encouragement:

> Incorporating a COIL collaboration into your existing course doesn't require an expensive technology platform or extensive redesign of your course. It requires an interest in innovative pedagogy, a bit of flexibility and enthusiasm, and some thoughtful preparation.[25]

As NAFSA, EVOLVE, and others have made clear, this "thoughtful preparation" begins with the training of the faculty partners, the "facilitators." The University of Michigan Virtual Exchange Initiative serves as an example of the kind of institutional support available to faculty. At the University of Michigan, I was provided with:

- An initial consultation with the directors of the Initiative to discuss my project, several months before the beginning of the fall semester's Italian diction class. Already, ideas for equipment and

Virtual Exchange 93

videoconferencing platforms were suggested. I was also given questions to ask my international partner about his and students' access to various digital technology.

- A series of weekly informational, interactive online Zoom workshops, beginning in mid-July, for both my partner and myself:

   Week 0: Preparations—Making sure the technology is working for you.
   Week 1: Introductions and Overview of Virtual Exchange
   Week 2: Instructional Models and Communication and Collaboration Tools
   Week 3: Task Design. Intercultural Learning Outcomes
   Week 4: Impact and Evaluation of Virtual Exchange
   Week 5: Finale Celebration

There were 21 University of Michigan faculty from different disciplines participating in these workshops, plus their foreign partners. Each workshop lasted two hours. Presentations by faculty who were already experienced in carrying out virtual exchanges were especially helpful.

- On-going check-ins during the semester by the Initiative to see how our exchange was going.
- A post-semester evaluation.
- A meeting with the original group of 21 teams to discuss our experiences.
- A meeting just before the following year's continuation of the virtual exchange.

Setting the Goals of a Virtual Exchange Diction Class: Hard, Digital, and Soft Skills

The goals of the class should be to facilitate the greatest outcomes of both hard diction skills and soft 21st-century skills, while carrying out best practice for diction pedagogy (see Chapter 2).

Through the very nature of an intercultural virtual exchange, hard and soft skills are intertwined; and, by definition, digital skills are enhanced in the process.

Hard Skills

The following student's comment, from a Stevens Initiative informational YouTube posting, is typical for virtual exchanges: "In virtual exchange, you really get to learn first and then apply what you

94 *Virtual Exchange*

learned..."[26] A similar comment comes from one of my own students: "I think this exchange is an extremely valuable endeavor. It was wonderful to synthesize the concepts we've been talking about throughout the term."[27] Thus, through work with native speakers, the hard skills of diction are placed in context and put into action beyond a typically compartmentalized classroom environment. Virtual exchange is a type of experiential, applied learning.

For our virtual exchange, Professor De Lisi's instructions to his Italian students were: "Give what is inside you when you hear the words and music of Italian songs and arias, because you are Italian and these are rooted in your family and your personal existence. Give the American students the opportunity to listen to those words with Italian ears."[28] One set of partners from our classes included American student Greta Groothuis, who worked with Italian student Paola Leggeri on "Qui la voce" from *I Puritani*. Groothuis said "I learned how important the language is to the overall effect of a piece. Paola emphasized emotion and how the diction contributes to emotion as much as dynamics and vibrato. Now I try to look more closely at the poetry and underlying meaning so I can master those facets before I get into the technical aspects. This will give me more confidence."[29] Leggeri sang two songs by African American composers, "Sweet Sorrow" by Maurice McCall, and "Love Let The Wind Cry... How I Adore Thee" by Undine S. Moore. "I fell in love with this beautiful music, although as an Italian I had never sung it before," said Leggeri. "Greta helped me correct my pronunciation and understand the meaning of English words and phrases. The music united us even though we are in two different cultures and working with two different repertoires."[30]

These comments illustrate how the exchanges are equal, and how soft and hard skills overlap and combine. For the American students, there is another hard skill at work. By working with Italians on their English diction, American students are compelled to think more about their own language, how they produce the sounds that come naturally to them, and how to explain their formation. Their critical listening skills are enhanced. At the same time, by listening so attentively to the Italians speaking and singing in English, they hear Italians' natural bright, forward placement and other innate tendencies, so that in the process, they are learning even more about Italian diction.

Greta Groothuis's comment about being more confident was echoed by an American tenor in my class who sang the Neapolitan song "O sole mio." He had been paired with an Italian who was thoroughly familiar with Neapolitan dialect. Now the American tenor sounds

Virtual Exchange 95

like an Italian tenor! Yet another American tenor sang a song from Ottorino Respighi's *Quattro rispetti toscani* and was ecstatic to receive feedback from Professor De Lisi, also a tenor, whose recording of Respighi songs he knew well. The whole class was enlightened—and their work placed in context—when they learned that the text to the song used a special Tuscan form of poetry, the *rispetto*, so that phrasal doublings were all the more essential for good pronunciation.

Professor De Lisi was pleased, too, with the hard skills his students had gained. The Italians had learned wonderful new repertoire with the direct collaboration of American singers, and they had advanced their skills singing in English, which would open up more job opportunities for them.

Besides the exchange of Italian and African American repertoire, my class involved short Mozart Italian recitative assignments, two people per mini-scene, in which Americans partnered with Italians. Since recitative is challenging for everyone, even when it is your own language, the benefit of this work was definitely not one-sided, and the Italians were happy to participate. The Italian students' future work, too, will involve performing many an Italian recitative with foreigners. As a young English speaker, imagine laying the groundwork for recitative by working one-on-one with a native Italian peer and performing it together!

These are just a few examples of the extremely valuable diction skills that students develop through a virtual exchange. The class enables singers to perfect individual sounds, while going way beyond this to real meaning and communication, getting to the heart of best practice for diction pedagogy. Critical listening skills, with a wide range of repertoire, are also enhanced.

Because the class is so hands-on and transformative, placing skills in context, students are so engaged that there is a much better retention of diction skills, and a huge motivation to develop them. What better way to meet the important best practice of laying the groundwork for a lifelong passion for language and communication than through virtual exchange, accessible to all?

Digital Skills

One of the skills that virtual exchange advances is digital competence. During the pandemic, of course, many singers became very adept with technology. We have to keep in mind, though, that a significant number of students deferred one or both semesters during the pandemic and did not get that kind of technological immersion. With a virtual

96 *Virtual Exchange*

exchange, students have the opportunity to use digital technology as a basic means of international collaboration.

Students working internationally communicate with one another through a variety of ways, and they naturally exchange ideas for how to communicate. For example, Facetime or Zoom; or asynchronously through Zoom video recordings; or audio recordings sent back and forth with comments. Quite a few European singers and pianists use WhatsApp on their smartphones, and this became a useful tool for some of our team partners. WhatsApp allows users to text, call, video chat, and send audio recordings from their phones.

The University of Michigan Virtual Exchange Initiative also researched web-based video annotation tools for us, such as VideoAnt and Annoto.[31] These tools allow viewers to write comments at specific points in the clips. The idea was that this might be useful for students giving feedback to one another. We might investigate this further, but so far students have been content just noting the specific timing within an audio or video clip, or simply referring in an email to the measure number, phrase, or words.

My new German diction exchange faculty partner created a group WhatsApp with her Italian partner, Professor De Lisi, that she calls *tandem linguistico,* after the bicycle built for two. She also offered to have the American students from my class join in. Her *tandem linguistico* is inspired by various language-study apps, such as Tandem, that connect pre-screened speakers around the world to help one another with language skills. Her WhatsApp *tandem linguistico,* however, is exclusive to members of her combined virtual exchanges. It enables voice students who worked together in the exchanges to keep in touch as a group and is completely voluntary. Students who opt in can network, and periodically send a message to the group asking for help with pronunciation in a song, the meaning of a phrase, repertoire suggestions, etc., or notify the group of an upcoming concert they are giving that will be live-streamed, or, truly, a limitless range of possibilities. Once again, the overlap with hard and soft skills is apparent.

Soft Skills

With the exchange, all my students' work was placed in context, they gained perspective, collaborated internationally, gained independence, forged new relationships, and crossed cultural boundaries. They grew exponentially because they were curious and engaged. And because they were so engaged, their retention is much greater.

Virtual Exchange 97

Everyone was taken outside of their compartmentalized environment, their work seen in context, with a widened perspective.

Some of the soft skills developed in a virtual exchange build on the skills listed at the end of Chapter 3. The skills listed there came from a diction class filled with diversity, including undergraduates working with graduates, and conductors and pianists working together with singers. Adding a well-facilitated virtual exchange element to this kind of class supercharges these skills and takes them to a global level:

- The greater perspective and international collaboration contributes to an atmosphere of cooperation and mutual respect.
- Students build greater communication skills, and important social skills for life outside of the school environment, as they will interact with people of all ages, backgrounds, and cultures.
- The class fosters inclusivity as students witness more and more diversity, and more variety of strengths and weaknesses, gaining empathy and understanding.
- Curiosity is stimulated, fostering openness, motivation, and initiative.
- Independence is developed, adding to students' confidence.
- The combined classes represent a mirror of the professional world the students will be entering. The interaction of younger and older; of singers, conductors, and pianists; of different cultures; of sharing languages and repertoires; with everyone sharing the same goals and interests—this helps give students a global outlook. In Chapter 5, we saw how students went from random exploration in their first year, to focused exploration in their second year—with a virtual exchange, this exploration extends well beyond their classroom.

The very nature of a song means that it is an expression of not only the composer and the poet, and of not only the performers, but that it is a door into another culture, and the time in history in which the song was written. The students in my classes saw our virtual exchange both as a great opportunity for working on Italian repertoire, and as a door into Italian culture and history. Likewise, the Italians fully embraced the beautiful art songs by African American composers with empathy and openness, as they, too, saw a great opportunity to learn about a whole different culture. With this part of the exchange—a true, equal cultural exchange—the unjustly neglected repertoire of African American composers was placed on equal footing with all other repertoire.

98   *Virtual Exchange*

Black Lives Matter: "Champions of This Music Should Look Like the Globe"[32]

News of the murder of George Floyd on May 25, 2020 resounded around the world. Protests in the United States began the next day. Protests outside the United States followed almost immediately thereafter and have now taken place in more than 60 countries on all seven continents.[33] There is no turning back—diversity, equity, inclusion, and active antiracism must permeate all that we do. There is much work to be done, and it cannot let up.

In 1977, Willis C. Patterson's eminent *Anthology of Art Songs by Black American Composers* was published.[34] As a master's student in collaborative piano at the University of Michigan in 1983–1985, I was fortunate to have my first exposure to some of the great songs in this anthology by playing for the voice lessons of several African American students in Willis Patterson's studio. It was wonderful repertoire, I learned a lot, and I placed the songs into my file of music labeled "American Art Song." It was, however, a long time before I truly realized that almost no one was singing these songs except African Americans, and that these wonderful works failed to appear in most American art song classes across the country, or on song recitals devoted to American music. As tenor George Shirley wrote in the Preface to the 1977 anthology: "While it is true that black composers have been published... it remains an indisputable fact that the social malady affecting our society has permitted only the tip of the iceberg to show."[35]

Gradually, more and more of the iceberg has been revealed, partly through the publication of more anthologies, such as *Art Songs and Spirituals by African-American Women Composers*, in 1995, compiled by Vivian Taylor;[36] Patterson's second anthology in 2002[37]; and *A New Anthology of Art Songs by African American Composers* in 2004, compiled by Margaret R. Simmons and Jeanine Wagner.[38] The most recent compilation is *An Anthology of African and African Diaspora Songs*, published in 2021 as part of the Videmus African American art song series, edited by Louise Toppin and Scott Piper; these songs were chosen specifically for the needs of the college singer.[39]

Dr. Louise Toppin's monumental online resource, *African Diaspora Music Project*, lists almost 4,000 works by composers of the African Diaspora.[40] Its mission is to create a repository of music; to provide access to scores; to encourage research, exploration, and performances of new works; and to assist student competitors in the annual George Shirley Vocal Competition in African American Vocal Repertoire.[41]

Virtual Exchange 99

As mentioned in Chapter 3, in 2007, singers Dr. Caroline Helton and Dr. Emery Stephens published their thought-provoking article "Singing Down the Barriers: Encouraging Singers of All Backgrounds to Sing Art Songs by African American Composers."[42] They expanded the article in 2019 for the important and timely book *So You Want to Sing Spirituals: A Guide for Performers*, by Randye Jones.[43] Their work, and others' work, along with the George Shirley Vocal Competition, held annually since 2011,[44] promotes the performance of African American vocal repertoire by *everyone*. This advocacy is summed up particularly well by Dr. Toppin:

> African American music is important for all of us to engage with because it tells a part of the narrative of American music, and without considering these narratives, we are teaching and singing an incomplete story of America. We need to have champions of this music, and champions of this music should look like the globe, not any one person, or any one race of people.[45]

At the University of Michigan, heeding Dr. Toppin's call that "champions of this music should look like the globe" began relatively early. From 1998 to 2010, the University of Michigan School of Music, Theatre & Dance offered a spring term abroad program for its voice students in Sesto Fiorentino, a short bus ride outside Florence, Italy. A diverse group of Michigan students sang their final concerts of the four-week program in the heart of Florence for an all-Italian audience. Each singer spoke to the audience in Italian, introducing their two songs—one an Italian song, and one an African American art song. Two cultures joined together, sending a strong message to both the singers and the very appreciative Italian audience. During that time, we also established ties with the Conservatorio Luigi Cherubini in Florence. As part of our cultural exchange, Italian voice students at the Florence conservatory learned and sang African American art songs for a masterclass with the great African American tenor George Shirley, while Professor Leonardo De Lisi presented a masterclass for Michigan students on Italian repertoire. This cultural exchange—in which the Italian and American students did not actually even meet one another, let alone collaborate—was the seed for the virtual exchange of 2020, which went far beyond an exchange of masterclasses. Without physically leaving our countries, the virtual exchange added global collaboration by having Italian and American students work together virtually one-on-one before performing for one another in the diction class virtual masterclasses. George Floyd's tragic death brought

100 *Virtual Exchange*

urgency, at a global level, to devote our attention to the study and performance of African American art song. It is absolutely fitting to present this vast, rich, neglected repertoire to our international cohorts as a representation of a very vital, significant part of America's music, poetry, history, and culture. In so doing, singers from both cultures learn and engage in dialogue, they are enriched, and they are then eager to share this unjustly neglected music with others.[46]

Because songs by African American composers are little known in Europe, it is certainly possible that your European partners will be hesitant to center their part of the exchange solely on this repertoire. If this seems to be the case, a first step in a virtual exchange, then, could be to assign some African American songs alongside other American repertoire by Leonard Bernstein, Aaron Copland, etc. On the other hand, Europeans may be very interested in the music of women composers, and songs by African American women composers can easily be introduced.[47] Also, some songs by African American composers can be introduced from the other direction, such as German songs by Robert Owens (see Chapter 3 "Equity: Whose Music Matters?"). After this initial exposure, European partners will most likely eagerly embrace more repertoire by African American composers in subsequent exchanges.

Canadians may want to introduce songs by the Black Canadian composer Robert Nathaniel Dett, and other Black Canadian composers listed on the website of the Canadian Art Song Project,[48] as well as songs by Indigenous Canadian composers, from the same site.[49] In the United Kingdom, the songs of the influential Black English composer Samuel Coleridge-Taylor are ripe for exchange, especially his *African Romances, op. 17,* seven songs composed in 1897 to the texts of the African American poet Paul Laurence Dunbar.

By having songs by African American composers be at the heart of a virtual exchange, we can expect these outcomes (in addition to hard diction and musical skills):

- Many, if not most, students in the United States are exposed to this repertoire for the first time. As an initial step, then, American students should read the seven-page article "Singing Down the Barriers" by Helton and Stephens.[50] As the American students study their assigned songs (that they will help their Italian partners learn), they gain knowledge about the repertoire and reflect about their own history and culture.
- As European students study the beautiful poetry and music of these songs alongside their American partners, they gain

understanding, insight, and empathy that go much deeper than the knowledge they might have already gained about American history and culture from their classrooms, movies, television, or the news.

- It is important to begin a dialogue about this neglected repertoire. The thoughtful, well-considered questions, insights, and comments that European faculty partners and students bring to the picture—the viewpoint of another culture—are very beneficial to the overall dialogue.
- George Shirley wrote of the African American art songs in Patterson's first anthology in 1977: "The songs herein speak of the human condition, therefore their appeal is universal."[51] The music and poetry speak for themselves, so that, as we have seen, European students embraced these beautiful songs wholeheartedly and were motivated to give them serious study. In doing so, the repertoire is placed on equal footing with the Italian repertoire that the American students had learned. The perspective that this gives to students on both sides really justifies the whole exchange.
- Of course, one outcome of this exchange is that performances of this repertoire will expand, both in the United States and in Europe, as "champions of this music should look like the globe."

Student Self-Evaluation, Feedback, and Reflection

Mary Lou Forward, the executive director of SUNY COIL, compares a virtual exchange to a study abroad program: "When you take students abroad, you do a predeparture orientation. With virtual exchanges... lack of preparation can derail the experience very quickly."[52] NAFSA explains:

> Whether they are classroom-based or focused on peer-to-peer conversations, meaningful experiences require intentional facilitation and authentic tasks. They also have structured components to help students prepare, work together, and then debrief after a project. And if the goal is to foster the same kinds of serendipitous experiences that come from in-person international learning, all these tasks—preparation, facilitation, collaboration, and reflection—must be more intentional.[53]

Another giant among virtual exchange programs is the Stevens Initiative. The Stevens Initiative was launched in 2015 by President Obama as the "Chris Stevens Virtual Exchange Initiative" to grow and

102 *Virtual Exchange*

enhance the field of virtual exchange between students of the United States, the Middle East, and North Africa. Although the work of the Stevens Initiative does not pertain directly to our lyric diction classes, the Initiative is committed to sharing best practices with the field and has published a helpful online toolkit, "Evaluating Virtual Exchange." For diction classes, this toolkit is beneficial for devising pre-exchange and post-exchange questions for students and is available at www.stevensinitiative.org.[54] Some examples, with a "strongly agree, strongly disagree" format, are:

> I like to learn about people from other cultures so that we can work together.
> I am confident that I can produce work with people from other places around the globe.
> I am able to adjust to new people, places, and situations.
> I can work productively with people whose cultural background is different from mine.

These and other questions are given both before and after the exchange. Just as the benefits of a diverse classroom, including mixed ages, are well-documented, so are the benefits of virtual exchange evidence based. This kind of feedback from students not only helps them get the most out of their exchange, but it also adds to the evidence base of virtual exchange, and specifically to our virtual exchange diction classes. It can help make the case for funding and can help shape diction curricula across the map.

Another resource for evaluating students' intercultural development is through the Association of American Colleges & Universities (AACU). The AACU seeks "to put culture at the core of transformative learning... The call to integrate intercultural knowledge and competence into the heart of education is an imperative born of seeing ourselves as members of a world community, knowing that we share the future with others."[55] Their "International Knowledge and Competence VALUE Rubric" highlights qualities that lie at the heart of a transformative 21st-century experience—empathy, curiosity, openness, and verbal and nonverbal communication.[56]

Still another resource is the book *Enhancing Learning through Formative Assessment and Feedback*, by Alastair Irons and Sam Elkington. The book advocates for a "return to focus on student learners," and "aims to encourage teaching and support staff to focus on the promotion of student learning through designing and embedding high-impact formative assessment processes and activities."[57]

Virtual Exchange 103

For African American repertoire, some questions may include:

Have you ever heard any art songs (other than spirituals) by African American composers before?
Have you ever studied or performed any art songs by African American composers before?
What insights did you gain from reading the article "Singing Down the Barriers: Encouraging Singers of All Backgrounds to Sing Art Songs by African American Composers?"

After the exchange, there should be a debriefing session with students from both countries, talking about what they have learned. For the African American component, a question to be asked of the American participants could be:

In terms of your personal understanding of the significance of African American art song as an expression of American culture and history, how did learning an African American song with a foreign peer—and helping this foreign colleague to perform the song—enhance your perspective as an American, and deepen your understanding?

Finally, the questions that appear at the end of this chapter, from philosopher Michael Sacasas, are thought-provoking and can be applied to any technology that students are using.

Longer Term Outcomes

The Stevens Initiative suggests following up with participants to learn about and document longer term outcomes. I am sure there is a domino effect for this kind of international collaboration, so that we cannot be aware of *all* of its far-reaching effects. For my recent virtual exchanges, I know that one of the Italian singers was cast in a production of *Peter Grimes* in Europe, so her American partner eagerly continued their collaboration in order to help her with the British pronunciation, which she knows. Another American/Italian pair are friends for life— they are both very creative crossover artists, which is one reason I had paired them up. One Michigan undergraduate has decided to apply to the Florence conservatory's master's program. One Michigan master's student is applying for a Fulbright award to study at the Florence conservatory, specifically hoping to build on the exchange begun in our diction class by studying both Italian repertoire and promoting songs

104 *Virtual Exchange*

by African American composers; another is applying for a Fulbright grant to study with my German partner in Nürnberg; and an outstanding Italian master's voice student is applying for the doctoral program at the University of Michigan.

Unbeknownst to us, while the Conservatorio Luigi Cherubini in Florence and the University of Michigan were carrying out our Italian/American exchange, the University of Florence was presenting a course on African American literature. When the Florence conservatory students performed an all-American song recital in Florence, which included the Italian premieres of the African American art songs, scholars from the University of Florence heard about it and learned that this was the result of study with Americans through virtual exchange. The University of Florence then invited Professor De Lisi and his students to join them for a symposium dedicated to African American literature. That symposium is planned as an annual event, and now the University of Michigan has been asked to join the two Florence institutions in these symposia. More and more collaboration, more and more diversity, dialogue, and perspectives—these are some of the longer term outcomes from virtual exchanges.

Final Words and More Questions: The Time Is Now

Many organizations across the globe are working to bring virtual exchange into the mainstream of higher education—Europe's EVOLVE, and the Erasmus+ program; the United States' NAFSA, COIL, and Stevens Initiative; APVEA (Asia Pacific Virtual Exchange Association); and others. For lyric diction classes, virtual exchange is one, clear answer for developing English-speaking singers' foreign language and diction skills, especially given their predominantly deficient background in foreign language study (see Chapter 5). Virtual exchange is also a powerful, equitable answer to cultivating intercultural, global, collaborative, and social skills for our relatively isolated students, while fostering their technological skills at the same time. Adding the purposeful study of African American art song can significantly help to fight racism while expanding the repertoire of performers across the United States and Europe.

A voice curriculum is unique, with its three skills of vocal technique, acting, and beautiful, communicative diction in at least several foreign languages, not to mention solid musicianship. The ability to carry out best practice in the teaching of all of these areas is essential for the education of our students. The time is ripe, and critical, for changes in academic curricula that will assure this ability, and more, helping to

Virtual Exchange 105

meet the needs of our students in our current century. In Chapter 1, I challenged us to ask the right questions—these can then guide the curricula, and not vice versa.

Michael Sacasas, writer, scholar, and philosopher on the ethics of technology, implores us to ask 41 questions of technology.[58] I list a few of his questions here for us to ask of the technology of virtual exchange. The answers, I believe, make clear that virtual exchange should become mainstream for our students. The answers they provide for diction classes are answers we need today:

> *What sort of person will the use of this technology make of me?*
> *What habits will the use of this technology instill?*
> *How will the use of this technology affect my experience of time? Of place?*
> *How will the use of this technology affect how I relate to other people?*
> *What knowledge has the use of this technology disclosed to me about myself? What knowledge has it disclosed to me about others? And is it good to have this knowledge?*[59]

As we quickly approach the end of the first quarter of the 21st century, then, the opportunity—and the urgent necessity—to break the mold of outdated administrative convenience and assumptions in our academic institutions lies squarely in front of us. The requirements of a singing actor are unique, and academic curricula must reflect the needs of today's voice students by allowing enough flexibility to support best practice in preparing singers for today's world at a global level. For diction classes, it is time to utilize the ideal tool of virtual exchange; it is time to take advantage of every opportunity to create the most diverse student body, including mixed age levels; it is time to avoid deficit teaching, compartmentalization, and siloing; and it is time to actively fight racism at every occasion. There is no turning back.

Notes

1. Used with permission. Marilou Carlin, "Retirements," *Michigan Muse* 40, no. 2 (Spring 2007): 37.
2. Penelope Cashman, "International Best Practice in the Teaching of Lyric Diction to Conservatorium-Level Singers" (PhD diss., Elder Conservatorium of Music, University of Adelaide, 2019), 312–313. Available at https://digital.library.adelaide.edu.au/dspace/handle/2440/120990.
3. "Virtual Exchange 101," *NAFSA*, June 4, 2020, https://www.nafsa.org/ie-magazine/2020/6/4/virtual-exchange-101.

106 *Virtual Exchange*

4. Ibid.
5. Directorate-General for Education, Youth, Sport and Culture (European Commission), "Erasmus+ 2021–2027," *Publications Office of the European Union*, March 23, 2021. Available at https://op.europa.eu/en/publication-detail/-/publication/ff1edfdf-8bca-11eb-b85c-01aa75ed71a1/language-en.
6. Ibid.
7. Leonardo De Lisi, at our initial meet-and-great class on October 12, 2020. Because of Brexit, however, the United Kingdom can no longer participate in Erasmus. The United Kingdom has initiated the "Turing Scheme" to replace Erasmus+. See Anthony Reuben and Tamara Kovacevic, "Turing Scheme: What is the Erasmus Replacement?," *BBC News*, March 12, 2021, https://www.bbc.com/news/education-47293927.
8. "Enrollment Trends," *Open Doors*, accessed July 10, 2021, https://opendoorsdata.org/data/international-students/enrollment-trends/.
9. "Number of International Students in the United States from 2004/05 to 2019/20, by Academic Level," *Statista*, accessed July 10, 2021, https://www.statista.com/statistics/237689/international-students-in-the-us-by-academic-level/.
10. For 2015–2016, 25% were in STEM fields, 20% were in Business and Management, and 17% were in Social Studies. "Study Abroad Data," *USA Study Abroad*, United States Department of State, accessed July 10, 2021, https://studyabroad.state.gov/value-study-abroad/study-abroad-data.
11. "Italian Language and Culture Courses," *Università per stranieri di Perugia*, accessed June 23, 2021, https://www.unistrapg.it/en/node/30.
12. "German for Singers," *Middlebury Language Schools*, accessed June 23, 2021, https://www.middlebury.edu/language-schools/languages/german/singers.
13. European Commission, Directorate-General for Education and Culture, "The Changing Pedagogical Landscape," accessed June 23, 2021, http://www.changingpedagogicallandscapes.eu/about-the-project/.
14. EVOLVE's website will stay up until 2026. "About Evolve," *EVOLVE*, accessed June 23, 2021, https://evolve-erasmus.eu/about-evolve/.
15. Ibid.
16. "Virtual Exchange 101."
17. But be careful of the time change around late October, when there is only a five-hour difference for about a week!
18. The line-up between Australia or New Zealand and Europe is more difficult. The fall session Down Under begins in March, which correlates with Europe's spring semester—this is fine, but the time zones are so far apart. It is still possible, though. For example, a class meeting in Sydney at 7 or 8 p.m. could line up with a European meeting at 11 a.m. or noon. Students' independent meetings outside of class require a lot of flexibility. It is well worth the effort! South Africa begins their academic year in early February, allowing a reasonable line-up with Europe's beginning in March.
19. "Virtual Exchange 101."
20. Email to the author, April 9, 2021. Used with permission.

Virtual Exchange 107

21. "List of Music Conservatories in Italy," *Wikipedia*, accessed June 3, 2021, https://en.wikipedia.org/wiki/List_of_music_conservatories_in_Italy.
22. "Category: Music Schools in Germany," *Wikipedia*, accessed June 3, 2021, https://en.wikipedia.org/wiki/Category:Music_schools_in_Germany.
23. "Category: Music Schools in Austria," *Wikipedia*, accessed June 3, 2021, https://en.wikipedia.org/wiki/Category:Music_schools_in_Austria.
24. "Category: Music Schools in France," *Wikipedia*, accessed June 3, 2021, https://en.wikipedia.org/wiki/Category:Music_schools_in_France.
25. *SUNY COIL*, accessed July 2, 2021, https://coil.suny.edu.
26. "What is Virtual Exchange?," *Stevens Initiative*, at *YouTube*, October 13, 2020, accessed May 18, 2021, https://www.youtube.com/watch?v=Kxun-F4cZPdw&t=138s, at 2:12.
27. Email to the author, November 12, 2020. Used with permission.
28. Claudia Capos, "Hearing with Italian Ears," published online July 7, 2021, as "Timothy Cheek's Virtual Exchanges Create a Bridge between His Italian Diction Students and their Italian Peers," accessed July 7, 2021, https://smtd.umich.edu/timothy-cheeks-virtual-exchanges-create-a-bridge-between-his-italian-diction-students-and-their-italian-peers/.
29. Ibid.
30. Ibid.
31. *VideoAnt*, University of Minnesota, College of Education + Human Development, accessed July 9, 2021, https://ant.umn.edu. *Annoto*, https://www.annoto.net, accessed January 20, 2022.
32. The quote is by Louise Toppin, in Waverly Long, "Bienen Releases First of Three Videos in Black Composer Showcase Series," *The Daily Northwestern*, July 13, 2021, accessed July 14, 2021, https://dailynorthwestern.com/2021/07/13/campus/bienen-releases-first-of-three-videos-in-black-composer-showcase-series/.
33. "List of George Floyd Protests Outside the United States," *Wikipedia*, accessed July 14, 2021, https://en.wikipedia.org/wiki/List_of_George_Floyd_protests_outside_the_United_States.
34. Willis C. Patterson, compiler, *Anthology of Art Songs by Black American Composers* (New York: Edwards B. Marks Music Company/Hal Leonard Corporation, 1977).
35. Ibid., iv.
36. Vivian Taylor, compiler, *Art Songs and Spirituals by African-American Women Composers* (Bryn Mawr, PA: Hildegard Pub. Co., 1995).
37. Willis C. Patterson, compiler, *The Second Anthology of Art Songs by African American Composers* (Ann Arbor, Michigan: Willis C. Patterson, 2002).
38. Margaret R. Simmons and Jeanine Wagner, compilers, *A New Anthology of Art Songs by African American Composers* (Carbondale, IL: Southern Illinois University Press, 2004).
39. Louise Toppin and Scott Piper, editors, *An Anthology of African and African Diaspora Songs* (Fayetteville, NC: Classical Vocal Reprints, 2021).
40. Louise Toppin, *African Diaspora Music Project*, https://africandiasporamusicproject.org.

108 *Virtual Exchange*

41. Louise Toppin, "About," *African Diaspora Music Project,* accessed June 3, 2021, https://africandiasporamusicproject.org/about-the-project.
42. Caroline Helton and Emery Stephens, "Singing Down the Barriers: Encouraging Singers of All Backgrounds to Sing Art Songs by African American Composers," *New Directions for Teaching and Learning,* no. 111 (Fall 2007): 73–79, available at https://deepblue.lib.umich.edu/bitstream/handle/2027.42/57353/288_ftp.pdf?sequence=1.
43. Emery Stephens and Caroline Helton, "African American Art Song," in *So You Want to Sing Spirituals: A Guide for Performers,* by Randye Jones (Lanham, MD: Rowman & Littlefield, 2019), 144–161.
44. *George Shirley Vocal Competition. African American Vocal Repertoire.* www.georgeshirleycompetition.com.
45. Long, "Bienen Releases First of Three Videos in Black Composer Showcase Series."
46. In his contribution to the *Emerging Fields in Music* series, Professor Edward W. Sarath, composer, writer, and performer, offers a future, built upon Black American music, for re-enlivening engagement with European classical music and launching an arts-driven revolution in creativity and consciousness, a vision that would compel education more broadly and to society at large toward being decidedly anti-racist. Edward Sarath, *Music Studies and Its Moment of Truth: Leading Change Through America's Black Music Foundations* (New York: Routledge, 2022).
47. For a start, see Taylor, *Art Songs and Spirituals by African-American Women Composers.*
48. Lawrence Williford, "Black Canadian Composers of Art Song," *Canadian Art Song Project,* August 4, 2020, accessed June 14, 2021, https://www.canadianartsongproject.ca/black-canadian-composers-of-art-song/.
49. Lawrence Williford, "Indigenous Canadian Composers," *Canadian Art Song Project,* September 29, 2020, accessed June 14, 2021, https://www.canadianartsongproject.ca/indigenous-canadian-composers/.
50. Helton and Stephens, "Singing Down the Barriers."
51. Patterson, *Anthology of Art Songs by Black American Composers.*
52. "Virtual Exchange 101."
53. Ibid.
54. For our purposes, the most helpful questions are under Group C: Cross-Cultural Communication and Cross-Cultural Collaboration (both Option 1 and Option 2), and Group E: Satisfaction and Prior Experience with Virtual Exchange. "Evaluating Virtual Exchange: A Toolkit for Practitioners," "Appendix: Common Survey Items for Virtual Exchange Programs," *Stevens Initiative,* updated July 2020, accessed July 2, 2021, in https://www.stevensinitiative.org/resource/evaluating-virtual-exchange-toolkit/.
55. "Intercultural Knowledge and Competence VALUE Rubric," *Association of American Colleges and Universities,* accessed June 12, 2021, https://www.aacu.org/value/rubrics/intercultural-knowledge.
56. "Inquiry and Analysis VALUE Rubric," *Association of American Colleges and Universities,* 2009, accessed June 12, 2021, https://www.aacu.org/value/rubrics/inquiry-analysis.
57. Alastair Irons and Sam Elkington, *Enhancing Learning through Formative Assessment and Feedback,* 2d ed. (New York: Routledge, 2021).

Virtual Exchange 109

58. "Transcript: Ezra Klein Interviews L.M. Sacasas," *New York Times*, August 3, 2021. https://www.nytimes.com/2021/08/03/podcasts/transcript-ezra-klein-interviews-lm-sacasas.html.
59. Ibid.

Bibliography

"About Evolve." *EVOLVE*. Accessed June 23, 2021. https://evolve-erasmus.eu/about-evolve/.

Capos, Claudia. "Hearing with Italian Ears." Published online July 7, 2021, as "Timothy Cheek's Virtual Exchanges Create a Bridge between His Italian Diction Students and their Italian Peers." Accessed July 7, 2021. https://smtd. umich.edu/timothy-cheeks-virtual-exchanges-create-a-bridge-between-his-italian-diction-students-and-their-italian-peers/.

Carlin, Marilou. "Retirements." *Michigan Muse* 40, no. 2 (Spring 2007): 37.

Cashman, Penelope. *"International Best Practice in the Teaching of Lyric Diction to Conservatorium-Level Singers."* PhD diss., Elder Conservatorium of Music, University of Adelaide, 2019. Available at https://digital.library. adelaide.edu.au/dspace/handle/2440/120990.

Directorate-General for Education, Youth, Sport and Culture (European Commission). "Erasmus+ 2021–2027." *Publications Office of the European Union*, March 23, 2021. Available at https://op.europa.eu/en/publication-detail/-/publication/ff1edfdf-8bca-11eb-b85c-01aa75ed71a1/language-en.

"Enrollment Trends." *Open Doors*. Accessed July 10, 2021. https://opendoorsdata.org/data/international-students/enrollment-trends/.

European Commission, Directorate-General for Education and Culture. "The Changing Pedagogical Landscape." Accessed June 23, 2021. http://www. changingpedagogicallandscapes.eu/about-the-project/.

"Evaluating Virtual Exchange: A Toolkit for Practitioners." Appendix: Common Survey Items for Virtual Exchange Programs. *Stevens Initiative*. Updated July 2020. In https://www.stevensinitiative.org/resource/evaluating-virtual-exchange-toolkit/Accessed on July 2, 2021.

George Shirley Vocal Competition. *African American Vocal Repertoire*. www. georgeshirleycompetition.com.

"German for Singers." *Middlebury Language Schools*. Accessed June 23, 2021. https://www.middlebury.edu/language-schools/languages/german/singers.

Helton, Caroline, and Emery Stephens. "Singing Down the Barriers: Encouraging Singers of All Backgrounds to Sing Art Songs by African American Composers." *New Directions for Teaching and Learning*, no. 111 (Fall 2007): 73–79. Available at https://deepblue.lib.umich.edu/bitstream/handle/2027.42/57353/288_ftp.pdf?sequence=1.

"Inquiry and Analysis VALUE Rubric." *Association of American Colleges and Universities*, 2009. Accessed June 12, 2021. https://www.aacu.org/value/rubrics/inquiry-analysis.

110 *Virtual Exchange*

"Intercultural Knowledge and Competence VALUE Rubric." *Association of American Colleges and Universities.* Accessed June 12, 2021. https://www.aacu.org/value/rubrics/intercultural-knowledge.

Irons, Alastair, and Sam Elkington. *Enhancing Learning through Formative Assessment and Feedback*, 2nd ed. New York: Routledge, 2021.

"Italian Language and Culture Courses." *Università per stranieri di Perugia.* Accessed June 23, 2021. https://www.unistrapg.it/en/node/30.

Jones, Randye. *So You Want to Sing Spirituals: A Guide for Performers.* Lanham, MD: Rowman & Littlefield, 2019.

Long, Waverly. "Bienen Releases First of Three Videos in Black Composer Showcase Series." *The Daily Northwestern*, July 13, 2021. Accessed July 14, 2021. https://dailynorthwestern.com/2021/07/13/campus/bienen-releases-first-of-three-videos-in-black-composer-showcase-series/.

Duffin, Erin. "Number of International Students in the United States from 2004/05 to 2019/20, by Academic Level." *Statista.* Accessed July 10, 2021. https://www.statista.com/statistics/237689/international-students-in-the-us-by-academic-level/.

Patterson, Willis C., compiler. *Anthology of Art Songs by Black American Composers.* New York: Edwards B. Marks Music Company/Hal Leonard Corporation, 1977.

—————. *The Second Anthology of Art Songs by African American Composers.* Ann Arbor, Michigan: Willis C. Patterson, 2002.

Reuben, Anthony, and Tamara Kovacevic. "Turing Scheme: What is the Erasmus Replacement?" *BBC News*, March 12, 2021. https://www.bbc.com/news/education-47293927.

Sarath, Edward. *Music Studies and Its Moment of Truth: Leading Change through America's Black Music Foundations.* New York: Routledge, 2022.

Simmons, Margaret R., and Jeanine Wagner, compilers. *A New Anthology of Art Songs by African American Composers.* Carbondale, IL: Southern Illinois University Press, 2004.

Stephens, Emery, and Caroline Helton "African American Art Song." In *So You Want to Sing Spirituals: A Guide for Performers*, edited by Randye Jones, 144–161. Lanham, MD: Rowman & Littlefield, 2019.

Stevens Initiative. "Evaluating Virtual Exchange: A Toolkit for Practitioners." "Appendix: Common Survey Items for Virtual Exchange Programs." Updated July 2020. Accessed July 2, 2021. In https://www.stevensinitiative.org/resource/evaluating-virtual-exchange-toolkit/.

—————. "What is Virtual Exchange?" At *YouTube*, October 13, 2020. Accessed May 18, 2021. https://www.youtube.com/watch?v=Kxun F4cZPdw&t=138s.

"Study Abroad Data." *USA Study Abroad.* United States Department of State. Accessed July 10, 2021. https://studyabroad.state.gov/value-study-abroad/study-abroad-data.

SUNY COIL. Accessed July 2, 2021. https://coil.suny.edu.

Virtual Exchange 111

Taylor, Vivian, compiler. *Art Songs and Spirituals by African-American Women Composers*. Bryn Mawr, PA: Hildegard Pub. Co, 1995.

Toppin, Louise. "About." *African Diaspora Music Project*. Accessed June 3, 2021. https://africandiasporamusicproject.org/about-the-project.

Toppin, Louise, and Scott Piper, eds. *An Anthology of African and African Diaspora Songs*. Fayetteville, NC: Classical Vocal Reprints, 2021.

"Transcript: Ezra Klein Interviews L.M. Sacasas." *New York Times*, August 3, 2021. https://www.nytimes.com/2021/08/03/podcasts/transcript-ezra-klein-interviews-lm-sacasas.html.

VideoAnt. University of Minnesota, College of Education + Human Development. Accessed July 9, 2021. https://ant.umn.edu.

"Virtual Exchange 101." *NAFSA*, June 4, 2020. https://www.nafsa.org/ie-magazine/2020/6/4/virtual-exchange-101.

Wikipedia. "Category: Music Schools in Austria." Accessed June 3, 2021. https://en.wikipedia.org/wiki/Category:Music_schools_in_Austria.

———. "Category: Music Schools in France." Accessed June 3, 2021. https://en.wikipedia.org/wiki/Category:Music_schools_in_France.

———. "Category: Music Schools in Germany." Accessed June 3, 2021. https://en.wikipedia.org/wiki/Category:Music_schools_in_Germany.

———. "List of George Floyd Protests Outside the United States." Accessed July 14, 2021. https://en.wikipedia.org/wiki/List_of_George_Floyd_protests_outside_the_United_States.

———. "List of Music Conservatories in Italy." Accessed June 3, 2021. https://en.wikipedia.org/wiki/List_of_music_conservatories_in_Italy.

Williford, Lawrence. "Black Canadian Composers of Art Song." *Canadian Art Song Project*, August 4, 2020. Accessed June 14, 2021. https://www.canadianartsongproject.ca/black-canadian-composers-of-art-song/.

———. "Indigenous Canadian Composers." *Canadian Art Song Project*, September 29, 2020. Accessed June 14, 2021. https://www.canadianartsongproject.ca/indigenous-canadian-composers/.

Index

accessibility *see* equity
Adams, David 45
African American composers 1,
9, 29–30, 81, 97, 98–101, 108n46;
women 29, 30
applied learning *see* experiential and
applied learning
asynchronous learning 6, 88, 89
autism 28

best practice in diction pedagogy
20–23, 72, 93, 95, 104
BIPOC 29
Black composers *see* African
American composers
Black Lives Matter 98–101
braille 28–29

Cashman, Penelope 18, 32–33; and
IPA 44–45; and vocal coaching
46–47
Castel, Nico 46, 49–50, 67
certification of diction instructors
21, 24n11
coachings, vocal 41, 46–47
COIL, SUNY 92, 101, 104
Coleridge-Taylor, Samuel 100
compartmentalization 19, 41,
71–73, 105; of first-year classes
58–59, 81
critical listening skills 22, 35, 94, 95
curricula: blurring of undergraduate
and graduate 32–35; for first-year
students 19–20, 56n10, 58–59,
60–61, 67, 73–74, 81; fixed 18,

31; flexible, 19, 31; free 19, 31,
69; graduate 20, 41, 42; mixture
19–20; for sophomores 58–59,
73–74, 81; undergraduate 16, 42;
see also deficit teaching; IPA,
introductory class

deficit teaching 64, 66, 105
DEI 1, 2, 27, 28; *see also* diversity;
equity; inclusivity
Dett, Robert Nathaniel 100
diagnostic tests 20, 41, 42
DictionBuddy 41, 53–54
diction pedagogy, best practice in
20–23, 72, 93, 95, 104
Diction Police, The 37n8, 53
differentiated teaching 27
digital skills, developing best use
of 22–23, 95–96; *see also* digital
technology
digital technology: audio and
video 37n8, 96; and braille 28–29;
and dictionaries and translators
51–52; and dyslexia 29; and
language tools 54; and memory
tools 54–55; and self-recordings
47–48; philosophy of ethics of
105; *see also* digital skills; virtual
exchange
diversity 2, 10, 19, 27, 81, 97,
102, 105; multi-age 31–37, 97,
102, 105
Doss, Mark S. 54, 63
Duolingo 54
dyslexia 29

Index 113

equity 29–30, 82, 95
Erasmus+ program 13n9, 84–87
experiential and applied learning 8, 74, 77n43, 81, 94

feedback, student 8–9, 91, 94; setting up 84, 101–103, 108n54
first-year students 19–20, 81; and language study 60–61, 67; and compartmentalization 71; *see also* curricula
Floyd, George 7, 98, 99–100

German language and diction 16, 23n4, 76n33, 85–86
graduate curricula *see* curricula: graduate; blurring of undergraduate and graduate
grammar study 61–67, 69, 75n15; and punctuation 61, 62, 66
Grubb, Thomas 15, 65

Helton, Caroline 29, 99, 100

inclusivity 28–29, 97
international collaboration *see* study abroad; virtual exchange
IPA (International Phonetic Alphabet) 8, 15, 16, 17, 19, 38n18, 40, 41, 42, 90–91; and braille 28–29; and dyslexia 29; introductory class 19, 56n10, 59, 64, 67, 69, 70, 81; pluses and minuses 44–46; *see also* Castel, Nico; DictionBuddy; Diction Police, The; IPA Source
IPA Source 46, 50–51, 52, 63
Italian diction, challenges of teaching 5, 13n5, 42, 67–68

Johnston, Amanda 23n4, 76n33

Katz, Martin 66

language learning tools 54
language study 59–60, 66–67, 81, 85
Leigh, Steven 24n11, 68–69

memory tools 54–55, 65–66
Montgomery, Cheri 17, 26–27, 28–29, 53, 75n22

NATS (National Association of Teachers of Singing) 4, 15, 21, 26; and NATS Hall Johnson Spirituals Competition 30

Owens, Robert 30, 100

Patterson, Willis C. 98
phonics 17, 56n10, 63
proficiency tests 20, 41, 42
punctuation 61, 62, 66

remedial classes *see* curricula, graduate
Renfro, Rebecca 28
review classes *see* curricula, graduate

Sacasas, Michael 105
scaffolded teaching 27
Shirley, George 30, 80, 98, 99, 101; voice competition 99
siloing 10, 42, 69, 76n36, 81, 105; of first-year students 58–59, 71–73; of K-12 students 76n36; of master's students 42, 72
skills: digital 22–23, 95–96; hard 81, 93–95; soft 11–12, 35–36, 81, 88, 96–97; *see also* digital technology
soft skills *see* skills, soft
sophomores *see* curricula, for sophomores
spaced repetition 54
Spanish 68
spirituals 29–30
Stapp, Marcie 13n5, 75n24
Stephens, Emery 29, 99, 100
study abroad 12, 82, 85
SUNY COIL 92, 101, 104
supplementary resources 22–23, 49–50; and DictionBuddy 54–55; and The Diction Police 53; and IPA Source 50–51; and Nico Castel 49–50; *see also* digital technology; language learning tools; memory tools

114   *Index*

Toppin, Louise 30, 98, 99, 107n32

undergraduate curricula *see*
  curricula

virtual exchange 1, 6, 30, 55;
  definition of 83–84; during
  sophomore year 74; equity in 30,
  95; and facilitator training 92–93;
  and faculty partners 91–92; and
  misgivings 88–91; and setting

goals 93; and time change 88–89,
  106n17, 106n18; *see also* skills
Virtual Exchange Initiative,
  University of Michigan 6, 7, 9, 83,
  92–93, 96
vocal coachings 41, 46–47

WhatsApp 96

YouTube 41, 48–49

Printed in the USA
CPSIA information can be obtained
at www.ICGtesting.com
LVHW012008041124
795688LV00046B/1478